THE Leadership GAP

**Dale F. Campbell
and Associates**

MODEL STRATEGIES FOR LEADERSHIP DEVELOPMENT

The American Association of Community Colleges (AACC) is the primary advocacy organization for the nation's community colleges. The association represents 1,100 two-year, associate degree–granting institutions and more than 10 million students. AACC promotes community colleges through six strategic action areas: national and international recognition and advocacy, learning and accountability, leadership development, economic and workforce development, connectedness across AACC membership, and international and intercultural education. Information about AACC and community colleges may be found at www.aacc.nche.edu.

Community College Press
American Association of Community Colleges
One Dupont Circle, NW
Suite 410
Washington, DC 20036

Printed in the United States of America.

ISBN 0-87117-346-8

CONTENTS

CONTRIBUTORS

Jacquelyn M. Belcher, District President, Georgia Perimeter College

Charles Carroll, Associate Vice President, Academic Affairs, Daytona Beach Community College, Florida

Daniel T. DeMarte, Assistant to the President and Executive Director of Planning, Macomb Community College, Michigan

Zelema Harris, President, Parkland College, Illinois

Cynthia Kachik, Assistant Director, 21st Century Educational Leadership Profiles Project, Institute of Higher Education, University of Florida

Albert L. Lorenzo, President, Macomb Community College, Michigan

Phyllis D. Montgomery, Director, Human Resources, Georgia Perimeter College

Carol Nasworthy, Trustee, Austin Community College, Texas

Frank William Reis, Executive Vice President, Human Resources and Administration, Cuyahoga Community College, Ohio

D. Kent Sharples, President, Daytona Beach Community College, Florida

Barbara Sloan, Vice President, Academic Affairs, Tallahassee Community College, Florida

FOREWORD

George R. Boggs
President and CEO
American Association of Community Colleges

Community colleges are unique among institutions of higher education because of their open-access mission, their responsiveness to community needs, their clear focus on student learning, and their entrepreneurial spirit. These colleges have developed a reputation for being flexible, innovative, and creative, and for responding to the educational and training needs of a changing society. The values that characterize the American community college movement were developed and implemented by visionary leaders. The continued success of these unique institutions will depend upon the quality and characteristics of their future leadership.

Many community college leaders and faculty members who joined community colleges during the growth years of the 1960s are now approaching retirement. In fact, 45 percent of presidents surveyed by the American Association of Community Colleges in fall 2000 indicated they would be retiring within the next six years. Perhaps even more alarming, administrators who normally would be logical choices to move into the presidency are also reaching retirement age. The average age of chief administrators reporting to college presidents is over 50.

This impending turnover in community college leadership is an obvious challenge to the institutions, but it is also an opportunity to bring greater diversity and new ideas into these positions. While the majority of community college presidents are male and Caucasian, the profile is changing. More than 34 percent of the presidents hired between 1995 and 1998 were female, and 15.7 percent were members of a minority group. Opportunities must be provided to encourage even more of our best people to prepare for positions of leadership. Mechanisms must be put in place to develop these potential leaders—leaders who are not afraid of change but who also embrace the community college mission and values. Future leaders must exhibit a passion for what our colleges do to help students make their dreams come true.

In *The Leadership Gap,* editor Dale F. Campbell and the chapter authors provide needed information on important aspects of college leadership. They address the importance of recruiting, selecting, orienting, and developing a diverse leadership team at a college and the methods to do so. They present models of ongoing leadership development programs at community colleges and how these programs benefit their colleges. The 21st Century Educational Leadership Profile is introduced as a tool to help in the selection and development of leaders and leadership teams.

The decisions necessary to operate a college require flexibility and timeliness; they cannot be made by a leadership team sitting around a table. For that reason, team members must have a common vision for their institution and a common set of values. But the most vital teams are those that bring a diversity of perspectives, skills, abilities, and talents to their assignments. Effective leadership teams do not come about by accident. They must be carefully selected and developed.

If community colleges are to meet the challenge of leadership turnover successfully, they will need the leverage implicit in a "grow your own leaders" model. Ideally, every community college president and chancellor should see the development of a new generation of leaders as an integral component of his or her job. Trustees should be sure that college policies encourage employees to engage in leadership development activities. Sabbatical leaves and tuition reimbursement programs are two significant incentives.

The Leadership Gap presents real-life college stories—models of what some colleges have learned about recruitment, selection, orientation, and development of leaders, and descriptions of how local leadership development programs and planning processes can be integrated. It is an essential book for those who care about the future of America's community colleges.

PREFACE

lthough each generation of community colleges has faced problems, the
challenges confronting the coming generation are particularly acute because
of the projected shortages of individuals qualified to assume community
college leadership roles in the next 10 years. Existing doctoral programs will not be
able to supply enough candidates to fill the anticipated demand. The problem is
receiving a great deal of attention in the field. For example, in March 2001, George R.
Boggs, president and chief executive officer (CEO) of the American Association of
Community Colleges (AACC), convened a national Leadership Summit to discuss the
issue and seek solutions.

This book suggests strategies colleges may use to address the coming leadership
shortage and to develop solutions to it. The book's intended audience includes community college trustees, CEOs, and other college executive officers. In Part I, college
executives who have created leadership development programs share some of the
lessons they have learned. In Part II, the authors focus on new tools available to
assist college executive officers engaged in leadership recruitment, selection, and
development.

Chapter 1 reviews the recent research on leadership development and describes
the work of a consortium that pilot tested the 21st Century Educational Leadership
Profile developed by the University of Florida Institute of Higher Education (IHE).
The chapter authors represent colleges that participated in the consortium and that
have used the Leadership Profile as part of their leadership development strategy.

Chapter 2 provides an overview of the leadership team selection, development,
and role expectations for administrators at Georgia Perimeter College, which oper-
ates under a shared governance model.

Chapter 3 summarizes the reflections of the chief executive officer at Parkland College in Illinois. It describes the positive changes that have occurred at Parkland as a result of investing in people and of involving the board of trustees in leadership development processes. The chapter highlights Parkland's annual President's Leadership Institutes, which have been instrumental in bringing about the transformation.

Chapter 4 discusses the Beacon Leadership Development Program, created by Daytona Beach Community College, Florida, in cooperation with the IHE. This partnership can serve as a model for community colleges that wish to join forces with university leadership development programs.

Part II begins in Chapter 5 with a review of three strategies used in recruiting and developing the leadership team at Macomb Community College in Michigan. The first strategy is an early leadership recruitment process called the Janus Program. The second is a method for assessing leaders and customizing professional development plans. The third is a performance appraisal process that aligns individual efforts with organizational goals.

Chapter 6 provides an overview of model strategies used at Cuyahoga Community College in Ohio to ensure diversity in faculty and staff. It features new Internet tools that can assist colleges in expanding applicant pools and expediting the hiring process.

Written from a trustee's perspective, Chapter 7 describes strategies used in hiring the president at Austin Community College in Texas. The chapter uses as examples two presidential searches. The experience may be helpful to trustees planning a search and to presidential applicants.

Chapter 8 reports on leadership profiles of the CEO and other cabinet executive officers at two colleges that have been recognized for their accomplishments in continuous quality improvement. The findings will be instructive for readers looking to identify essential attributes for current and future community college leaders.

Chapter 9 offers recommendations to those involved in leadership recruitment and development, and a list of resources.

We hope readers will benefit from the lessons learned by these authors. For community colleges today, no task is more important than nurturing and developing strong and effective leaders.

Dale F. Campbell

ACKNOWLEDGMENTS

This book was a collaborative effort from its inception. I owe a great deal to the following friends and colleagues:

- George R. Boggs, president and chief executive officer of the American Association of Community Colleges (AACC), and the AACC Board of Directors for convening the National Leadership Summit and making leadership development a priority of the association.

- Chapter authors for their support of the 21st Century Educational Leadership Profiles Project and participation in the User's Group.

- Jerome Wartgow, former president, Colorado Community College and Occupational Education System, for funding Colorado as a pilot. His support enabled us to begin to collect normative data for the Profiles Project and to conduct further research in this area.

- SHL for its leadership in human resources management. SHL's research in work profiling provided the framework for the development of the 21st Century Educational Leadership Profile.

- University of Florida higher education administration doctoral students, who used the Leadership Profile and the Occupational Personality Questionnaire (OPQ) Job–Match to identify areas for further improvement in their leadership development efforts.

- D. Kent Sharples, president, Daytona Beach Community College, Florida, for his commitment to leadership development in partnering with the University of Florida Institute of Higher Education to sponsor the first Beacon Leadership Program.

- Dan Moore, Sam Morgan (deceased), Don Rippey, John Roueche, Ed Boone, and Terry O'Banion, all of whom have been my mentors.

- Community college leadership development programs conducted at universities and sponsored by associations. Community college presidents nationally who mentor faculty and staff and invest in their professional development.

- The new generation of current and emerging leaders who have a passion for and commitment to the community college mission in the 21st century.

PART I

LEADERSHIP

DEVELOPMENT

CHAPTER 1

Leadership Profile Research and Consortium

Dale F. Campbell, Professor and Director, Institute of Higher Education, University of Florida, and Cynthia Kachik, Assistant Director, 21st Century Educational Leadership Profiles Project, Institute of Higher Education, University of Florida

The changing demographics in the United States are signaling severe shortages in the country's management ranks. The Bureau of Labor Statistics (2001) projects that such shortages will occur as baby boomers near retirement and the average age of the workforce rises.

Community colleges, which experienced a growth spurt in the 1960s, are particularly susceptible to this management shortage. A 2001 American Association of Community Colleges (AACC) Leadership Survey indicated that 45 percent of community college chief executive officers (CEO) will retire within the next six years, and another 34 percent will be retiring within the next seven to 10 years (Shults 2001, 1). In fact, all levels of higher education are experiencing a relatively high turnover rate among presidents (Padilla and Ghosh 2000). College and university presidents in the United States typically serve only five to seven years at an institution (Kerr and Gade 1986; McLaughlin and Riesman 1990; Ross and Green 1998). Filling these anticipated vacancies requires immediate planning.

Studies indicate that most failures among new executive hires occur because personalities do not mesh, not because the executives are incompetent (Greene 1999). Increasingly, candidates for executive positions in many fields are being asked to take personality assessments as part of the interview process (Grensing-Pophal 2000). These tests are used to determine how well a candidate will fit into an organization's culture. The major purpose of this chapter is to present information about selecting administrators with personality characteristics that may be appropriate to the community college culture. Assessing individual fit is an extremely important factor in leadership development and selection.

Personality Traits and Leadership Effectiveness

Early research on leadership looked at the role of personality traits as predictors of leadership effectiveness. It did not result in the development of a consistent set of traits that differentiate leaders from nonleaders or effective leaders from ineffective leaders (Goldberg 1993). A movement away from the personality trait approach led to the exploration of behavioral characteristics of leaders, contingency models of leadership, and the role of the situation (Bass 1990). Recently, in light of the limitations in contingency and situational theories, there has been renewed interest in the relationship of personality traits to leadership (e.g., Gough 1990; Grensing-Pophal 2000). Research on emergent theories of leadership shows that personality is an important variable in leadership identification and development (Silverstone 2001) and that consideration of measures of personality can add significantly to the prediction of job performance (Bain and Mabey 1999; Barrick and Mount 1991).

Presidential search processes have often guided colleges and universities to hire presidents who fit a particular profile. An important line of research since 1970 has been to study the profile of sitting presidents (Barr 1981; Ferrari 1970; Green 1988; Mancini 1993; Ross and Green 1998; Vaughan 1990; Vaughan and Weisman 1998; Weisman and Vaughan 2002). These studies usually followed the same pattern; they examined the demographics (e.g., gender, age, educational attainment, marital status) of persons already in the position but did not include a study of personality characteristics. Nicholson (1996) concluded a discussion of personality–environment fit by stating that personality should be described in profile terms to determine how persons fit teams or cultures of an organization. This chapter reports on our efforts to build on this research base by developing a profile of the personality attributes of those in community college administration.

The Profiles Project

The 21st Century Educational Leadership Profiles Project began in 1995. It was developed by the Institute of Higher Education (IHE), University of Florida, in cooperation with Saville & Holdsworth Ltd. (now SHL). The purpose of the project was to develop a profile of a public community college president working in an on-demand learning environment (Campbell and Leverty 1997). The personality assessment used to develop the Leadership Profile was based on the Occupational Personality Questionnaire (OPQ) from SHL. The OPQ is a behavioral questionnaire developed for use in selecting, developing, and establishing career paths in business (Saville &

Holdsworth 1996). SHL has helped more than 5,000 clients, including 62 Fortune 100 companies, use the OPQ to hire employees.

The OPQ Concept 5.2 version is a 248-item graphic rating scale. For each item, participants are asked to indicate on a five-point Likert-type scale the degree to which they strongly disagree (1) to strongly agree (5). An example of one item is "I like to get every detail right." The results are reported as raw and sten scores on each of 30 personality dimensions measured by the OPQ and are based on research into behavioral differences across a wide range of jobs. The OPQ is a self-report measure of personality and behavioral characteristics that are particularly relevant to the world of work. Research has shown that predictive validity of the OPQ measure of job performance ranges from 0.29 to 0.38 when a job analysis is conducted (Saville & Holdsworth 1996).

The Profiles Project (Campbell and Leverty 1997) created an Attribute-Based Person–Job Match Report that generated 19 characteristics ranked as Essential, Important, or Other Relevant on the basis of the 30 OPQ characteristics. Three Essential characteristics (Data Rational, Critical, and Forward Planning), an Important characteristic (Traditional), and the Other Relevant characteristics for community college presidents are shown in Table 1.1.

The first phase of the project consisted of a consortium of 12 community colleges that used the OPQ either for professional development of staff or for selection decisions. Consortium participants to date are Austin Community College (Texas), Cleveland Community College (North Carolina), Clovis Community College (New Mexico), Contra Costa Community College (California), Cuyahoga Community College District (Ohio), Dallas County Community College District (Texas), Georgia Perimeter College, Macomb Community College (Michigan), Madison Area Technical Institute (Wisconsin), the North Carolina Community College System, Palm Beach Community College (Florida), and Parkland College (Illinois).

Jacquelyn M. Belcher, district president of Georgia Perimeter College, joined the project in 1999. Her incentive was largely financial. She noted, "When we hire a senior administrator at $100,000, with an average of 4 percent increase annually, at the end of three years the cost to the college is $400,000. At the end of six years, it has compounded to $877,000. And at the end of 30 years, the investment would be $7,300,000." The implications of hiring the wrong person are staggering financially and, equally important, they could cause campuswide disruptions. The Leadership Profiles Project provides tools to assist colleges in personnel selection and professional development programs.

Table 1.1
OPQ Attributes

Attribute	Low Level of Attribute	High Level of Attribute
T2 – Data Rational	Judges on basis of intuition	Judges on basis of data/logic
F6 – Critical	Accepts points without question	Critically evaluates ideas
T9 – Forward Planning	Operates without preplanning	Enjoys forming short-term plans
		Enjoys forming long-term plans
T5 – Traditional	Prefers nontraditional work culture	Follows conventional approach
R6 – Socially Confident	(No lower level for this attribute)	Is confident with people
T4 – Behavioral	Avoids analyzing others' behavior	Likes analyzing others' behavior
T10 – Detail Conscious	Leaves details to others	Is concerned about details
R1 – Persuasive	Dislikes persuading/negotiating	Can sell and be persuasive
R2 – Controlling	Prefers others to take control	Prefers to direct or take control
F9 – Achieving	Wants security more than success	Is ambitious for success
R8 – Democratic	Decides without consultation	Consults others before deciding
F1 – Relaxed	Worries about work problems	Can switch off work pressures
R9 – Caring	Tends to disregard people issues	Is empathetic and tolerant
T7 – Conceptual	Avoids theoretical approaches	Enjoys working with theory
T6 – Change Oriented	Seeks little change/variety in work	Seeks change/variety in work
R5 – Affiliative	Prefers to work alone	Likes to work with groups/teams
T8 – Innovative	Sticks to prevalent ideas/solutions	Enjoys creating novel solutions
F5 – Optimistic	Expects the worst to happen	Keeps an optimistic outlook
F4 – Emotional Control	Communicates with emotion	Keeps feelings hidden

Source: Saville & Holdsworth 1996.

Participants in the consortium meet at least once annually. In addition, a liaison appointed by each college participates in User's Group meetings during the year, typically in conjunction with the Community College Futures Assembly in February and the AACC Annual Convention in April. User's Group lessons include matching the Leadership Profile to the culture of the institution; communicating the proper use of the OPQ; proper interpretation of OPQ results; and using OPQ results to structure individual development plans for the CEO, trustees, human resources officers, and other members of the leadership team.

Profiles Project Participants

The community college leadership database for the first phase of the project consisted of 294 community college administrators. Fifty-seven percent (169) came from 13 states (Arkansas, California, Colorado, Georgia, Illinois, Michigan, Missouri, New Mexico, North Carolina, Ohio, Texas, Washington, and Wisconsin). Forty-three percent (125) of the subjects were administrators at Florida community colleges. The community college administrators' database consisted of 141 (48 percent) women and 153 (52 percent) men.

The community college administrative participants in the study took the OPQ either online or using paper and pencil between August 1996 and May 2001. Participants received a report showing attribute sten scores from 1 to 10, based on norm tables. Over the course of the study, norm tables were updated; consequently, for consistency in data comparisons, all data were converted to raw scores ranging from 4 to 36. The study sample was initially contained in Excel spreadsheets and imported into an SAS data set for statistical analysis.

Results

Figure 1.1 illustrates the results of the average attribute scores of the study participants as well as averages for female and male administrators. The profile of scores shows that the administrators scored lowest on Traditional (T5), indicating they preferred a nontraditional work culture. High scores on Change Oriented (T6) and Innovative (T8) indicated they sought change/variety in work and enjoyed creating novel solutions. Low scores for Emotional Control (F4) indicated they communicated with emotion. Higher scores on Affiliative (R5) and Socially Confident (R6) indicated that the participants liked to work with groups/teams and were confident with people.

The highest scores for administrators were on Optimistic (F5), meaning they kept an optimistic outlook. This finding corresponded with the fairly high scores for Persuasive (R1), Affiliative (R5), and Socially Confident (R6). The participants' scores were average for Relaxed (F1). High scores for Caring (R9) indicated the administrators were empathetic and tolerant of others. This characteristic corresponded with fairly high scores for Affiliative (R5), Democratic (R8), and Behavioral (T4).

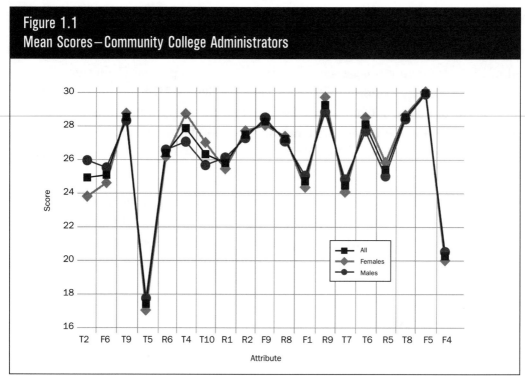

Figure 1.1
Mean Scores—Community College Administrators

*See Table 1.1, page 6, for list of OPQ attributes.

Gender Studies

A major goal of the Leadership Profiles Project is to collect data with ongoing research to develop community college leadership norms and to perform gender studies. In SHL gender studies based on corporate management norms, the OPQ suggested that males tend to be somewhat more Data Rational and Traditional, while females are more Change Oriented (Saville & Holdsworth 1996). These results are consistent with those reported in psychological literature (Ashmore and Sewell 1998).

Some contemporary researchers working in the social sciences report that women display specific gender-based leadership characteristics (Belenky, Clinchy, Goldberger, and Tarule 1986; Gilligan 1982; Grogan 1996; Helgesen 1990; Noddings 1992; Shakeshaft 1989). Gillett-Karam's (1994) work on behavioral characteristics of community college leaders revealed that effective leadership is more behaviorally derived than gender based and that leadership is subject to the dynamics and interactions of people and institutions. In Gillett-Karam's view, leadership depends on situations, not gender.

Acebo (1994) has a slightly different perspective, viewing the community college leader as a team leader. Acebo encourages community college leaders to bring shared leadership and accountability into focus within their organizations. She compares and contrasts established leadership models in her work but argues that efforts to create dynamic teams with "synergy," a form of group energy, are part of the paradigm shift taking place in leadership styles.

Desjardins (1994) focused on Gilligan's (1982) work and stressed that differences are gender related but not gender specific, with more men found in the Justice/Rights orientation and more women in the Care/Connected orientation.

For the Profiles Project study, researchers used the standard 0.05 alpha significance level to analyze variance. Only 4 of the 19 characteristics showed significant differences between the genders. The Data Rational (T2) attribute was significantly different (p = 0.00), with males ($\overline{X}$ = 25.97) scoring higher than females ($\overline{X}$ = 23.82); this difference suggested that the men judged on the basis of data/logic more than the women did. The Behavioral (T4) attribute was significantly different (p = 0.00), with females ($\overline{X}$ = 28.75) scoring higher than males ($\overline{X}$ = 27.08), suggesting that the women liked analyzing others' behavior more than the men did. The Detail Conscious (T10) attribute was significantly different (p = 0.03), with females ($\overline{X}$ = 27.04) scoring higher than males ($\overline{X}$ = 25.69), suggesting that the women were more attentive to details than the men were. Finally, the Caring (R9) attribute was significantly different (p = 0.01), with the females ($\overline{X}$ = 29.75) scoring higher than the males ($\overline{X}$ = 28.85), suggesting that the women were more empathetic and tolerant of others than the men were.

Discussion

The first phase of the Profiles Project had some limitations. Study participants were in management positions by title, but no representation was made with respect to their leadership styles or effectiveness. Also, the study was based largely on self-report responses that subjects might distort, particularly on personality measures, to create a favorable impression (Barrick and Mount 1996). Some data were collected when participants were job applicants; at such a time, they could be motivated to employ impression-management tactics and threaten the purposes of the personality measurement (Rosenfield, Giacalone, and Riordan 1995). Internal validity threats to this study were lack of uniformity in test administration (paper-pencil versus online) and the fact that participants took the tests over several years and that the sample populations used in the study may not be representative of the population. There might also have been confounding variables in studying personality, such as age, specific aspects of the job, and the type of institution.

Nonetheless, the first-phase results may assist persons aspiring to leadership positions to assess their capacity for management on the basis of theories of personality. Awareness of one's own personality characteristics and those of others has been recognized as important for individual professional development and for work in teams.

Some member colleges of the Profiles Project use OPQ reports to study leadership styles and team styles of their management group. Presidents from Leadership Profiles Project's consortium colleges share the lessons they have learned in the next chapters to assist colleges interested in replicating and strengthening their leadership development and selection programs.

References

Acebo, S. 1994. "A Paradigm Shift to Team Leadership in the Community College." In *Handbook on the Community College in America: Its History, Mission, and Management,* ed. George Baker. Westport, Conn.: Greenwood Press, 580–588.

Ashmore, R. D., and A. D. Sewell. 1998. "Sex/Gender and the Individual." In *Advanced Personality,* eds. D. F. Barone, M. Hersen, and V. B. Van Hasselt. New York: Plenum Press, 377–408.

Bain, N., and B. Mabey. 1999. *The People Advantage: Improving Results through Better Selection and Performance.* West Lafayette, Ind.: Ichor Business Books.

Barr, Clifford V. 1981. "Profiles of American College Presidents—1968 and 1980: A Comparison." Doctoral dissertation, Bowling Green State University. *Dissertation Abstracts International* 42–04A: 1386.

Barrick, M. R., and M. K. Mount. 1991. "The Big Five Personality Dimensions and Job Performance: A Meta-Analysis." *Personnel Psychology* 44: 1–26.

Barrick, M. R., and M. K. Mount. 1996. "Effects of Impression Management and Self-Deception on the Predictive Validity of Personality Constructs." *Journal of Applied Psychology* 81: 261–272.

Bass, B. M. 1990. *Bass and Stogdill's Handbook of Leadership: Theory, Research and Managerial Applications.* 3d ed. New York: Free Press.

Belcher, J. 2000. "The Leadership Network: Mentoring the Current Team and Selecting New Partners." Presentation at 2000 American Association of Community Colleges Annual Convention. 10 April, Washington, D.C.

Belenky, M. F., B. M. Clinchy, N. R. Goldberger, and J. M. Tarule. 1986. *Women's Ways of Knowing.* New York: Basic Books.

Bureau of Labor Statistics. 2001.
  http://www.bls.gov/opub/ooq/oochart.htm.

Campbell, D. F., and L. H. Leverty. 1997. "Developing and Selecting Leaders for the
  21st Century." *Community College Journal* 67: 34–36.

Desjardins, C. 1994. "Leadership and Gender Issues in the Community College." In
  Managing Community and Junior Colleges: Perspectives for the Next Century, eds.
  A. M. Hoffman and D. J. Julius. Washington, D.C.: College and University
  Personnel Association, 147–161.

Ferrari, M. R. 1970. *Profiles of American College Presidents*. East Lansing, Mich.:
  MSU Business Studies.

Gillett-Karam, R. 1994. "Women and Leadership." In *Handbook on the Community
  College in America: Its History, Mission, and Management*, ed. George Baker.
  Westport, Conn.: Greenwood Press, 94–108.

Gilligan, C. 1982. *In a Different Voice: Psychological Theory and Women's
  Development*. Cambridge, Mass.: Harvard University Press.

Goldberg, L. R. 1993. "The Structure of Phenotypic Personality Traits." *American
  Psychologist* 48: 26–34.

Gough, H. G. 1990. "Testing for Leadership with the California Psychological
  Inventory." In *Measures of Leadership*, eds. Kenneth E. Clark and Miriam B. Clark.
  West Orange, N.J.: Leadership Library of America, 355–379.

Green, M. 1988. *The American College President: A Contemporary Profile*. Washington,
  D.C.: American Council on Education.

Greene, J. 1999. "Head Games." *Hospitals and Health Networks* 73(6): 52–54.

Grensing-Pophal, L. July 2000. "Who Are Your 'Next Generation' Leaders?" White
  paper. Alexandria, Va.: Society for Human Resource Management.

Grogan, M. 1996. *Voices of Women Aspiring to the Superintendency*. Albany: State
  University of New York Press.

Helgesen, S. 1990. *The Female Advantage*. New York: Doubleday.

Kerr, C., and M. L. Gade. 1986. *The Many Lives of Academic Presidents: Time, Place
  and Character*. Washington, D.C.: Association of Governing Boards.

Kline, P. 1993. *Personality: The Psychometric View*. London: Routledge.

Mancini, D. D. 1993. "Career Paths to the Academic Presidency: A Comparison
  Study of Gender Differences." Doctoral dissertation, Bryn Mawr College.
  Dissertation Abstracts International 54–12A: 4610.

McLaughlin, J. B., and D. Riesman. 1990. *Choosing a College President: Opportunities and Constraints.* Princeton, N.J.: The Carnegie Foundation for the Advancement of Teaching.

Nicholson, N. 1996. "Towards a New Agenda for Work and Personality: Traits, Self-Identity, 'Strong' Interactionism, and Change." *Applied Psychology: An International Review* 45(3): 189–205.

Noddings, N. 1992. *The Challenge to Care in Schools: An Alternative Approach to Education.* New York: Teachers College Press.

Padilla, A., and S. Ghosh. 2000. "Turnover at the Top: The Revolving Door of the Academic Presidency." *The Presidency* 3(1): 30–37.

Rosenfield, P., R. A. Giacalone, and C. A. Riordan. 1995. *Impression Management in Organizations.* London: Routledge.

Ross, M. R., and M. F. Green. 1998. *The American College President.* Washington, D.C.: American Council on Education.

Saville & Holdsworth Ltd. 1990. *Occupational Personality Questionnaires Manual and User's Guide.* Boston: SHL.

——. 1996. *Occupational Personality Questionnaires Manual and User's Guide.* Boston: SHL.

Shakeshaft, C. 1989. *Women in Educational Administration.* Newbury Park, Calif.: Corwin Press, Inc.

Shults, Christopher. 2001. *The Critical Impact of Impending Retirements on Community College Leadership.* Research Brief Leadership Series, no. 1, AACC-RB-01-5. Washington, D.C.: American Association of Community Colleges.

Silverstone, C. 2001. "Leadership Effectiveness and Personality: A Cross-Cultural Evaluation." *Personality and Individual Differences* 30: 303–309.

Vaughan, G. B. 1990. *Pathway to the Presidency: Community College Deans of Instruction.* Washington, D.C.: Community College Press, American Association of Community Colleges.

Vaughan, G. B., and I. M. Weisman. 1998. *The Community College Presidency at the Millennium.* Washington, D.C.: Community College Press, American Association of Community Colleges.

Weisman, Iris M., and George B. Vaughan. 2002. *The Community College Presidency 2001.* Research Brief Leadership Series, no. 3, AACC-RB-02-1. Washington, D.C.: American Association of Community Colleges.

SHL provided data regarding the test–retest reliability and internal consistency reliability data of the OPQ that were critical in deciding to use the instrument. The job interview normally used in selection has poor test–retest reliability; in some cases the reliability was little better than 0 (Kline 1993). A correlation coefficient of 0.70 or more between the two testings is generally preferred (Kline 1993). The test–retest reliability coefficients for the OPQ scales, based on a student sample (N = 86) with a one-month interval between testings, ranges from 0.69 for Critical (F6) to 0.94 for Outgoing (R4), with a median of 0.84 (Saville & Holdsworth 1990).

Internal consistency reliability was measured using Cronbach's alpha providing an estimate of the correlation of the set of test items with another set of similar items from the same collection of items, with 0.70 being regarded as a minimum figure for an adequate test (Kline 1993). Item responses from 441 managers were used to estimate the internal consistency reliability of the OPQ scales using Cronbach's coefficient alpha. The coefficients ranged from 0.53 for Independent (R3) to 0.88 for Practical (T1) and Data Rational (T2). Internal consistency reliability (coefficient alpha) of OPQ scales has a median of 0.75 (Saville & Holdsworth 1990).

SHL (1990) addressed validity issues in using the OPQ for job selection in terms of relative validity of assessment methods, with 1.0 representing the perfect prediction of job success. It has been shown that no single assessment method comes close to this. Assessment center approach scores 0.6, work sample tests score 0.46, occupationally relevant ability tests and personality questionnaires score 0.40, structured interviews score 0.35, unstructured interviews score 0.25, and references alone score 0.10 (Bain and Mabey 1999, 37).

When using these measures for job-selection purposes, most people use a mix of methods. However, the more thorough the process in this regard, the more it is likely to cost. With finite budgets and time, most companies tend to rely merely on the interview. It is hard to see how any thorough recruitment exercise could be implemented without an interview. This method, however, is not without fault; issues arise over the speed at which conclusions are drawn about candidates, as well as about the possibility of interview bias or subjectivity, when it is used alone. In reality, the interview should be accompanied by other methods.

The OPQ has been subject to criterion and construct validation. Criterion-related validation studies have found it to be a valid predictor of job performance across a range of managerial jobs, including banking, insurance, manufacturing, airlines, service firms, and high-tech industry. The OPQ has also been correlated against popular personality inventories such as the 16 PF, the Myers–Briggs Type Indicator, Gordon Personal Profile, and the DISC (Saville & Holdsworth 1990). Results of the construct validation studies suggest that the OPQ measures essentially what it intends to measure.

The Profiles Project is a continuing study, and the consortium and User's Group remain active. Current plans include expanding the project nationally and allowing additional colleges to join the consortium. Contact information and additional resources about the Profiles Project can be viewed online at http://www.coe.ufl.edu/Leadership/Distance/leaders/project/profproj.html.

CHAPTER 2

Leadership Team Selection and Development

Jacquelyn M. Belcher, District President, and
Phyllis D. Montgomery, Director, Human Resources,
Georgia Perimeter College

What is the magic of leadership? How do you find the right magicians for your leadership team? Can old magicians learn new tricks?

Faced with a serious shortage in leaders, many institutions are asking themselves these questions. As seasoned administrators are retiring and the average tenure in upper-level positions is getting shorter, community colleges face the challenge of finding new leaders for their administrative teams.

At Georgia Perimeter College we found ourselves confronting these challenges in 1999, when the provost of our Clarkston Campus retired and we began the search for his replacement. This chapter recounts our experience during that period.

The Setting

The organizational structure of Georgia Perimeter College and its shared governance method of operation present unique challenges for the selection and development of the institution's administrative team. The Board of Regents of the University System of Georgia has developed a tiered system of colleges and universities to best meet the varied needs of the citizens of the state. Some graduate universities specialize in academic research; other institutions focus on teaching. Georgia Perimeter College is a teaching institution.

Georgia Perimeter College is the largest two-year associate degree–granting institution in the University System of Georgia. It serves more than 19,000 students at six regional campuses and centers; however, each location maintains an individual, small college atmosphere. Decentralized administration encourages each location to cater to the needs of its particular student body.

The College Executive Team (CET) includes the president, the executive vice president for financial and administrative affairs, the vice president for academic and student affairs, and the executive assistant to the president for advancement and external affairs, all of whom have districtwide responsibility, as well as four campus provosts.

For many years, the college operated under a traditional, centralized administration model. In 1996, a shared governance model was introduced (Figure 2.1).

Figure 2.1
Shared Governance Policy

Consistent with the policies of the Board of Regents, it is the policy of Georgia Perimeter College that decisions should be made in consultation with those affected, that participation in governance bodies should be broad-based, and that communication with respect to decision making should be available to the entire College Community. Georgia Perimeter College recognizes the value of diverse opinions in decision making and pursues its mission in an atmosphere of shared governance and open communication. Faculty, staff, and administrators recognize their shared accountability for the performance of the College in carrying out its mission. All members of the College community must be accountable for their roles.

Under the shared governance policy, some operational areas remain centralized under the district vice presidents; however, most administrative responsibilities have been decentralized to the campus level. In addition, policymaking activities and other administrative issues are now shared by representatives of the entire college community through a series of assemblies, boards, councils, and a faculty senate (Figure 2.2).

Figure 2.2
Shared Governance Bodies

- College Advisory Board
- Faculty Senate
- Professional and Administrative Staff Assembly
- Support Staff Assembly
- Academic Affairs Policy Council
- Student Affairs Policy Council
- Institutional Effectiveness Policy Council
- Human Resources Policy Council
- Administrative Services Policy Council
- Information and Instructional Technology Policy Council

Launching the Search Process: Key Considerations

As we began to search for a new provost, we were keenly aware of the importance of a successful search and of the challenges involved in finding the right candidate for the position. We recognized that there is an increasing shortage of effective leaders and that competition is great. We also knew that the search process would be costly. Several thousand dollars would be required for advertising and travel costs; in addition, there would be personnel costs associated with service on the selection committee.

Potentially even more costly, in terms of productivity, morale, and institutional image, would be the repercussions associated with making a poor choice. Many of us have had the experience of hiring an individual to fill a leadership position and later finding, to our dismay, that the fit was not right. At best, resolving such a situation entails a great deal of additional leadership development; at worst, it leads to a costly termination process and even the possibility of litigation.

We knew it would be essential to find an individual who was not only highly qualified but also right for our institution. We knew that all the candidates would likely have been in leadership positions in organizations; they would have leadership potential as well as leadership experience. But how many of them would be the right fit for the leadership role we wished to fill, namely, to lead a team at an institution that operated under a nontraditional shared governance model? What individual traits might be related to successful leadership in these circumstances?

We recognized that evaluating a candidate's experience and performance alone would not give us enough information upon which to make our decision. We also recognized the importance of considering all the factors involved in leadership, especially as they relate to the structure and governance of the organization. In our case, the provost holds some of the responsibilities typically assumed by a chief executive officer; however, he or she must also be capable of being a team member in the district organization. In addition, the shared governance philosophy requires a capacity for participatory management.

Elements of the Search Process

With these considerations foremost in mind, we developed the plan for our search. Our plan included traditional methods, such as a review of the candidates' professional credentials, reference checks, and interviews. We also decided to add a new dimension to our plan. Accepting the theory that measures of personality may provide information that is predictive of behavior in professional as well as personal situations, we decided to evaluate our six finalists using information from the 21st Century Educational Leadership Profile. The profile uses information provided by the candidates to assess how they would work with a team, how they would perform as leaders, and how they would respond in a subordinate role.

Many of us have had the experience of hiring an individual to fill a leadership position and later finding, to our dismay, that the fit was not right.

Because of Georgia's governance structure and the unique demands it places on our top leaders, we were particularly interested in the third category of the profile— Subordinate Behavior. We felt that the Subordinate Behavior area would provide useful information about how each candidate might be expected to work with our president. More specifically, we felt that candidates who scored high as Self-Reliant, Collaborating, and Informative could be expected to fit the needs of the college.

The profile of the candidate who was ultimately selected for the position provided useful information about how he could be expected to face the challenges of the position. This information, combined with the traditional selection processes, increased our confidence that we had made a good choice for the college.

Developing and Mentoring the Leadership Team

Defining the needs of the institution and identifying the individuals who are best suited to meet those needs are important steps in leadership development. However, the most important factor in enhancing leadership in the organization is the ongoing development and mentoring of the leadership team. At Georgia Perimeter College, we have identified five components that we believe are important to this process:

1. Evaluating the institutional environment

2. Learning about the current leadership team

3. Continual environmental scanning

4. Ongoing leadership team evaluation and training

5. Looking internally for new leaders

Evaluating the Institutional Environment

All higher education institutions have many things in common; however, the unique characteristics of each college or university have the most significant impact on leadership needs. Leadership styles that work well in one place may fall flat in another. For this reason, forming a leadership philosophy and selecting and developing a leadership team begin with an institutional environmental scan. At Georgia Perimeter College, we looked at three areas—(1) our position in the higher education community; (2) our organizational structure; and (3) our mission, values, and vision—as we began to plan programs and processes to maximize the effectiveness of our leadership team.

With respect to our position in the higher education community, we are a large, nonresidential, two-year, regional, multicampus college within the University System of Georgia. We serve diverse populations of traditional and nontraditional students in greater metropolitan Atlanta. We share with all other institutions in the Georgia University System the following characteristics:

■ A supportive campus climate, necessary services, and leadership and development opportunities, all to educate the whole person and meet the needs of students, faculty, and staff

■ Cultural, ethnic, racial, and gender diversity in the faculty, staff, and student body, supported by practices and programs that embody the idea of an open, democratic, and global society

- Technology to advance educational purposes, including instructional technology, student support services, and distance education
- Collaborative relationships with other system institutions, state agencies, local schools and technical institutes, and business and industry; sharing physical, human, information, and other resources to expand and enhance programs and services available to the citizens of Georgia

Our decentralized organizational structure and our shared governance administrative model offer many challenges for our leadership team. It is important that team members be both independent and cooperative. The provosts must not only provide leadership for their individual campuses but also be sensitive to districtwide issues. The vice presidents must be responsible for collegewide decision making yet be responsive to the unique needs of each campus.

With respect to our mission, values, and vision, we see ourselves as a community committed to learning and to becoming a preeminent associate degree–granting institution. Faculty, staff, administrators, and students aspire to gain national recognition as a community of learners and to assume a national leadership role in developing creative, technologically advanced academic and student services programs. Our vision also includes serving as a model for developing partnerships to deliver public services, technical assistance, lifelong learning, and education and training in response to the needs of diverse collegiate and community constituencies. Further, we are committed to diversity, continuous improvement, high academic standards, and the efficient use of resources. Enhancement of our students' lives is our first priority.

Learning about the Current Leadership Team

Having identified who we were and what we hoped to be, we set out to assess the strengths and weaknesses of our current leadership team. In 1999, the president asked the members of the CET to take the Occupational Personality Questionnaire. Their responses were matched to the 21st Century Educational Leadership Profile and culminated in the development of a Person–Job Match Report for each team member. We were also provided with the Expert Occupational Personality Questionnaire Report, which summarizes the individual's own view of his or her behavior. The Person–Job Match Report compared the knowledge, skills, and competencies of each team member with those required to be successful as an educational leader in the 21st century. The Expert Occupational Personality Questionnaire Report provided insights into the individual's relationships with others, along with thinking styles, feelings and emotions, and behavior styles.

After we had collected information related to the personality and leadership style of each member of the CET, the next step was to determine how we could use that information to maximize leadership effectiveness. Like other community colleges, we highly value teamwork, communication, change orientation, forward planning, and the ability to compromise. The profiles varied widely. For example, the profile of one team member indicated a nonparticipative, low-negotiative, moderately adaptable management style, while another team member was highly participative, highly negotiative, and highly adaptable.

Such information has helped us better understand how CET members work together, how they approach administrative issues, and how they work with their individual management teams. It also provides direction for planning and monitoring collective and individual team development experiences. In the annual individual evaluations with the president, team members have the opportunity to collabora-tively identify their professional growth needs as well as evaluate progress. The full team is involved in designing the collective approach to assessing its group dynamics. Each team member assumes responsibility for participating in enhancing the effec-tiveness of the college leadership.

Continual Environmental Scanning

An effective leadership development program includes continual environmental scan-ning. Mindsets such as "That's the way we have always done it" or "Things were better in the old days" can spell disaster for institutions. Environmental change must be anticipated and accommodated.

As a state institution, we must remain aware of political changes, such as a new governor or state legislators. We have to be sensitive to fluctuations in the economy and in community educational needs. We must plan programs that are responsive to rapidly changing technology, and we must ensure an ongoing analysis of our strengths, weaknesses, opportunities, and threats. We need a team that can provide effective leadership in response to environmental changes.

Ongoing Leadership Team Evaluation and Training

It is also important to continually assess the members of the CET and to offer them opportunities to enhance their effectiveness as individuals and as team members. Professional development programs enable staff members to find satisfaction and meaning in their work; at the same time, they ensure that the college has a corps of leaders whose talent and energy it can tap. The importance of customizing programs to meet individual needs cannot be overemphasized. Education and training packages may include college-sponsored programs as well as programs designed by external sources.

Georgia Perimeter College's approach to individual development begins with the premise that effective leadership is derived from an acceptance of the human condition and an appreciation of human potential. We seek to empower our leaders by focusing on their strengths instead of their weaknesses. When motivation is external, people perform only for the reward. Sustained peak performance must be internally inspired.

Integral to intrinsic motivation is the need for appropriate feedback. This feedback also includes rewards, which we provide at the college and the unit levels. As part of this process, it may be useful to modify the way in which jobs are designed to create engaging, engrossing work that motivates leaders to perform at peak levels.

Ongoing assessment also provides information essential to planning appropriate leadership development programs. The 21st Century Educational Leadership Profile has a work-profiling system that includes an individual development planner. This tool helps each person identify priorities and develop an action plan. It also provides a follow-up procedure to review the effectiveness of the development activities.

Participation in national leadership programs has been very beneficial for individual team members' development. We have found Staub Leadership Consultants' HILS (Helping Individuals Lead Successfully) Seminar to be beneficial for the entire team. Some members have attended the League for Innovation in the Community College's Executive Leadership Institute, as well as the Harvard programs and the National Institute for Leadership Development. We use our annual College Executive Team retreat as a time to bring in recognized authorities on leadership as well as to focus on institutional planning and team-building activities. At our 2001 annual CET retreat, team members spent the first day assessing their personal interaction styles and examining effective leadership strategies. During the remaining four days, a process observer with experience in personality assessment and in higher education administration joined the group and provided continuous feedback related to the group's interaction. The information derived from this experience will continue to inform the process of executive team building.

Looking Internally for New Leaders

The most effective members of the CET were promoted internally. Promotions enhance staff morale. Moreover, these leaders' knowledge of the history of the institution, their loyalty to and pride in the college, and the respect of their colleagues are valuable assets.

In 2000, at the request of the president, staff of our human resources department developed a weeklong leadership program for college staff at all levels. The agenda includes individual personality assessment, group activities, and presentations on issues such as team building, trust, diversity, and college-related information. The program not only has accomplished its original goals but also has produced other significant changes for the college, including a dramatic improvement in morale. Participants feel empowered. Because the program brings together staff members from different campuses and areas of responsibility, it has significantly improved campuswide communication. There is a great sense of family and increased understanding of how their positions affect the college and its mission. The participants have expressed appreciation for the opportunity to learn more about the role of the president and other members of the executive team who have participated in the program. Participants also appreciate the opportunity to express their feelings, concerns, and ideas to top-level administrators.

As a result of this program and other activities directed toward identifying and developing leadership internally, we are feeling the excitement of new ideas and innovation all around the college.

Conclusion

Is there magic in leadership? Yes, there is. However, leadership also requires a great deal of hard work and a little luck. At Georgia Perimeter College, we have found creative ways to maximize the effectiveness of our leadership team. These techniques give us an advantage when addressing the leadership shortage that higher education institutions now face. Through the continued use of strategies for identifying leaders and potential leaders and implementing programs for continual development of our leadership team, we expect to be able to meet the leadership challenges ahead.

CHAPTER 3

Commitment to Leadership Development Begins with the CEO

Zelema Harris, President, Parkland College

Parkland College, located in Champaign, Illinois, is a publicly supported institution that opened in 1967. Since its inception, the college has enjoyed community support. For example, in 1968, voters approved, by a three-to-one margin, a $7.5-million bond issue for the construction of the permanent campus.

When I arrived on campus as president in 1990, the college still was held in high esteem by the community. However, internally, all was not well. The college faced severe financial problems. Money had been pulled from the education fund to complete a costly construction project, and the college's fund balance of more than $7 million was depleted. The college's founding president had retired in 1987. A new president was brought in with much acclaim and expectation. Several staff positions, as well as programs, were eliminated. Employees joined unions out of fear of losing their jobs. After two years, the president was forced to retire in the midst of controversy and anger.

An Institution Ready for Transformation

Parkland was an institution clearly in need of transformation. It was equally clear that the needed transformation had to come from within. My experience as a community college president taught me that institutional transformation is a result of investing in people. Parkland had a proud history; many of its faculty and staff had been at the college from the beginning. While they recognized the need for change, they wanted to be part of the process. Seeking to put in place a collaborative leadership style, I created an Executive Team to help lead the college. I soon found, to my surprise, that faculty were initially concerned that a "committee" was now making decisions. Previously, when a faculty member needed a decision, he or she just had to go to the vice president. Before a truly collaborative environment could be established, additional groundwork would be needed.

Subsequent conversations with longtime faculty revealed the depth of their concern. Faculty were unclear about where the college was going. This conversation led to a one-day leadership retreat. I was convinced, however, that more was needed to bring about a transformation at Parkland. We needed a model for leadership development.

Finding the Right Leadership Model

After reviewing several leadership models, we selected the model developed by Jeff Hockaday, then chancellor of Pima Community College District in Arizona. Hockaday's model was designed to prepare community college leaders for presidencies. Although I was more interested in developing leaders at all levels throughout our college, I could see that his approach was solid and that it could be adapted to Parkland's needs. With so many faculty and staff approaching retirement over the next five to 10 years, it was important that we start building an internal pool of leaders.

Hockaday came to Parkland as a consultant. He met with faculty and staff and became familiar with our campus culture. As we began to create the leadership program, he asked what we wanted it to accomplish. I replied that I wanted our people to have a good understanding of the community college movement and our mission. I also wanted them to see how Parkland fit into the national community college picture. In addition, I believed it was important for them to gain skills and knowledge in organizational development, budget planning, conflict resolution, and the role of a board in college governance. In keeping with input from faculty, however, our chief aim was to give faculty and staff a grasp of how decisions are made at Parkland and how they could be involved in planning and decision making for Parkland's future.

With these goals in mind, we began to design an agenda for a leadership institute that would be the springboard for Parkland's new leadership development program. We named the seminar "Leadership: A Commitment to Involvement in the Decision-Making Process of Parkland College." It was scheduled for May 25–27, 1994, at a conference center in nearby Monticello, Illinois.

Planning the First Leadership Seminar

Developing the Agenda

We asked David Pierce, then president of the American Association of Community Colleges, to present a national perspective on community college issues. The executive director of the Illinois Community College Board at that time, Cary Israel, provided the statewide community college perspective. George Vaughan summarized the research on community college leadership.

We also invited a panel of highly effective community college presidents to share their experiences. Each president identified the leadership skills he or she considered important for faculty and staff. The panel format also gave the seminar participants a firsthand look at different leadership styles.

> With so many faculty and staff approaching retirement over the next five to 10 years, it was important that we start building an internal pool of leaders.

To achieve one of our chief goals—namely, to show faculty how they could be involved in planning and decision making—we chose to focus on an important and extremely sensitive issue, budget planning. Staffers become far more accountable when they understand such factors as the impact of enrollment or of health insurance increases on the institution's bottom line.

Selecting Participants

With the program and speakers in place, we needed to select participants. We decided to limit attendance at this first event to 20 persons, and we wanted the majority of participants to come from the faculty. For this reason, we reserved 15 slots for faculty.

We mailed letters of invitation to all full-time faculty, staff, and administrators. We received more than 50 applications. We selected 20 people, who represented a balanced mix in terms of departments, gender, and years of experience at the college. It was difficult to leave people out, but we made a commitment to faculty and staff that we would offer the seminar every year as long as there was interest in attending.

Results of the First Seminar

Feedback from the seminar participants was overwhelmingly affirming. The session on budget planning was especially well received.

To me, the response of one individual was particularly gratifying. He had written me soon after my arrival at Parkland and expressed his general discontent. He wrote, "The college is going downhill and I'm sick about it. I speak for the silent majority."

This faculty member was one of three participants we asked to share their thoughts at the conclusion of the seminar. To my great relief, he exclaimed that he had never felt so cared about during his more than 20 years at Parkland. While I also believed that the seminar had been effective, I never anticipated such a strong, positive reaction, particularly from someone who had formerly expressed such discontent.

Two things became clear: the seminar must continue, and the leadership potential among the faculty and staff ranks was enormous.

Making a Good Seminar Better

We made two important changes to the 1995 seminar. First, we extended the length of the session by one day. Second, we held the 1995 session at a conference center farther off campus, so participants would be obliged to stay overnight. Both of these changes made the seminar even better. There was more time to discuss issues and more time for the participants to bond with each other and with the seminar speakers.

The seminar has been held annually since its inception. We have continued to fine-tune the logistics, the program, and every aspect of the seminar. We always ask participants to complete a written survey before they leave, and we have used many of their suggestions to improve the seminar.

Over the years, some of the most respected community college professionals have participated in the seminars. We have changed the seminar topics to meet evolving faculty concerns and needs. For example, the current program includes a session on ethics and core values in the community college. Presenting this session is Donald Phelps, W. K. Kellogg Regents Professor and Professor in the Community College Leadership Program at the University of Texas at Austin.

Another recent addition to the program is a session on individual leadership styles. The participants take the Myers–Briggs Type Indicator prior to arriving at the seminar, and their scores are interpreted and discussed during the program. It is important for all the participants to know themselves and to understand how they can best provide leadership for the college. This exercise also demonstrates that there is no single "best" leadership style.

An important component of the seminar has been the reading materials we provide the participants prior to the seminar (see sidebar). With one exception, the selections change each year. We always ask participants to familiarize themselves with a document commonly referred to as the Truman Commission Report (President's Commission 1947). Although this report was published a half-century ago, a more cogent description of the community college mission would be hard to find.

Selected Seminar Readings

- Bensimon, Estela M., and Anna Newmann. 1993. *Redesigning Collegiate Leadership: Teams and Teamwork in Higher Education.* Baltimore, Md.: Johns Hopkins University Press.
- Kennedy, Gail. 1952. *Education for Democracy: The Debate over the Report of the President's Commission on Higher Education.* Boston: Heath.
- Boggs, George R., et al. 2001. "Community Colleges at a Crossroads." *Presidency* 4(1): 14–21.
- Kidder, Rushworth M. 1995. "There's Only Ethics." In *How Good People Make Tough Choices.* New York: William Morrow; 177–208.
- Roueche, John E., and Suanne D. Roueche. 1998. "Dancing as Fast as They Can— Community Colleges Facing Tomorrow's Challenges Today." *Community College Journal* (April/May): 30–35.
- Gleazer, Edmund J., Jr. 1980. *The Community College: Values, Vision and Vitality.* Washington, D.C.: Community College Press, American Association of Community Colleges.
- Harris, Zelema, and Pauline E. Kayes. 1997. "From Policy to Action: Parkland College's Implementation of North Central's Statement on Access, Equity, and Diversity." *NCA Quarterly* (spring): 451–456.
- Harris, Zelema. 1995. "A Journey Worth Taking: Transformational Quality and Leadership." *Community College Journal* (April/May): 32–36.
- McCabe, Robert H. 2000. *No One to Waste: A Report to Public Decision Makers and Community College Leaders.* Washington, D.C.: Community College Press, American Association of Community Colleges.
- President's Commission on Higher Education. 1947. *Higher Education for American Democracy.* Washington, D.C.: U.S. Government Printing Office.

The Seminars' Benefits

Parkland has made a significant investment in the leadership seminars during the past eight years. The cost, excluding staff time, is about $20,000 per year. How do we know if it works? Do we now have more leaders than we did in 1994? Is the program relevant?

The benefits may be examined from two important perspectives—that of the faculty and that of the board.

Faculty

Since 1994, 176 faculty, staff, and administrators have participated in the seminar. They include 100 women and 76 men. Thirty have been people of color.

More than 35 seminar alumni hold leadership positions throughout the college. Some have moved from the faculty ranks to become department chairs and associate vice presidents. Others chair task forces and committees. Several have initiated innovative projects in online learning, mentoring, diversity, retention, crisis management, and other areas.

> We always ask participants to familiarize themselves with a document commonly referred to as the Truman Commission Report.

Many alumni remain in their original positions but have expanded their roles by becoming leaders in their own spheres. For example, one alumna observed that whenever her department chair asks for volunteers to take on new tasks and responsibilities, the hands that go up always belong to leadership alumni.

In essence, we have created a pool from which we can draw candidates for the many positions that will become available at Parkland in the near future.

Board of Trustees

An unexpected benefit of the leadership seminars has been the increased involvement of our board of trustees. Since the first seminar, we have invited the chair of our board and other officers of the board to speak to seminar participants about the board's role.

Our trustees have responded enthusiastically to this opportunity to create a new connection with our faculty and staff. Moreover, participants have been impressed by the knowledge and dedication of our board members, who are elected by district constituents and receive no financial compensation for serving on the board.

Our trustees have been inspired to have their own short retreat during our seminar. They spend an afternoon with a facilitator discussing trusteeship and the role of the board. Then they join us for dinner and make their presentation in the evening.

Taking Leadership Development One Step Farther

We recognize the importance of offering ongoing leadership development for faculty and staff who have attended the seminars. For example, we are using the 21st Century Educational Leadership Profile created by Dale Campbell to assist us with the transition of leadership. The Leadership Profile is a proactive response to the changing of the guard, as many of our veteran leaders, including department chairs and administrators, retire. Individuals who take the Leadership Profile are asked to develop personalized leadership objectives on the basis of what they learn from its results.

Another example of ongoing leadership development occurred when a group of leadership alumni voluntarily came together to find ways to better integrate experienced faculty with new faculty. This effort has evolved into a strong faculty mentoring program at Parkland. In addition, we convened a leadership alumni Futures Conference in 1997. This conference was the first time that all the alumni had met together as one group.

A key activity at the Futures Conference was to "create a community college of the future." Looking back on the ideas that emerged at that session, it is satisfying to recognize that in many ways, Parkland has created the community college of the future. For instance, our leaders visualized a college that was open 24 hours a day, 7 days a week. With the college's extensive offerings of online learning, Parkland is always open for business.

Recently, the leadership alumni were invited to attend a special session with George Boggs, an invited speaker at our 2001 leadership seminar. His topic was "The Learning College."

John Roueche was the keynote speaker at our 2002 Futures Conference, an event that serves as the kickoff to Parkland's ongoing strategic planning process. Leadership alumni were invited to attend this event and to participate in the planning process.

These special events and activities not only provide continual professional development but also instill a sense of community among the leadership alumni.

I work most effectively when I understand the big picture. The retreat gave me the opportunity to place the work I do for Parkland into a larger context. For me, that was both affirming and motivating. I felt better about the contributions I had made and envisioned new ways I could make a difference in the future.

The Leadership Program...started me thinking about education as more than a classroom endeavor. It provided me with a deeper understanding of how the institutional culture and organization works. Concepts such as planning, budgets, and the role of the Board of Trustees were largely a mystery to me before attending the retreat. Most important, the Leadership Program offered me the opportunity see our singularity of purpose. Before attending, I saw the roles of administrators, faculty, and staff as being distinct from one another. The emphasis placed on the mission and purposes and our common goals, however, allowed me to begin thinking about our roles in the institution as integrated and complementary. In a sense, leadership is not a function of what position we serve in the college, but how we realize the college's mission within that position.

Before I attended the leadership conference, I was at a crossroads in my career.... The conference reminded me why I had initially chosen to work at a community college and why I remain at Parkland—the mission, the leadership, the academic programs, the talented staff, and the diverse students.

The days spent with my colleagues fostered collaborative relationships across the college that continue to be helpful when accomplishing college initiatives, problem-solving on behalf of my students, and even the nitty-gritty everyday tasks.

The Leadership Conference was the capstone event in a year that altered the course of my professional life.... By the end of the conference, I knew that I would make a career of the community college and that I wanted to give to Parkland as much as it was giving to the community...a direct outcome of the Leadership Conference was my choice to work toward an Ed.D. in community college leadership.

Leadership Development and the CEO: Final Thoughts

I believe the most significant decision I have made since assuming the presidency at Parkland is to develop the leadership program. The program has created a college of leaders who understand our mission—not the words, but the passion. Many ideas for improving student learning had their genesis at the conferences. The collegiality among faculty and staff is an unexpected long-term benefit. This is not to say that challenges do not exist or that faculty members no longer disagree with the president. However, it does mean there is an openness that allows these issues to be addressed.

If every community college employee knew more about his or her own college's history and the history of the community college movement and understood that we are not restricted by our job titles or by employee groups, I believe we could rise to new heights in serving our students. Unfortunately, I am also convinced that many colleges still view organizational development as an "add on" that can be discarded when resources are tight or not even considered when things are going well. They fail to recognize that we are in the business of student learning, and those of us who serve this function must also be engaged in our own professional development and the development of our institution.

To build a community of leaders at Parkland, we knew we had to create an environment that supports excellence, fosters growth, and includes everyone. I believe we have created such an environment. As one of the leadership alumni has said, "There is a spirit of renewal, excitement, and energy."

Beacon Leadership Program

D. Kent Sharples, President, and Charles Carroll, Associate Vice President, Academic Affairs, Daytona Beach Community College

The final test of a leader is that he leaves behind him in other men the conviction and will to carry on.

—WALTER J. LIPPMANN (1945)

In my interview for the presidency of Daytona Beach Community College (DBCC), I shared my opinion that a first-rate leader surrounds himself or herself with first-rate people, and a second-rate leader surrounds himself or herself with third-rate people. Nurturing and developing leadership skills is an essential responsibility of the college president.

Although DBCC had an excellent faculty and staff, the college had not emphasized leadership development over the years, and many good people had held the same positions for several years. Employees often left the college without having realized their leadership potential. This was an institutional as well as a personal loss. The absence of a leadership development program significantly reduced the likelihood that leaders would emerge from within to help move DBCC forward.

Changing the Culture: First Steps

The college's culture was based on a strong, centralized leadership approach. With our new leadership development program, we sought to create a system that would welcome broad-based input and use a problem-solving approach. We started by creating a Planning Council composed of 30 members, half of whom were faculty members. This group was charged with reaching a consensus on college planning activities. The council had nine committees: Teaching and Learning, Enrollment

Development, Instructional Program Review, Administrative Unit Review, Technology, Human Resources, Diversity, Operations, and Strategic Planning.

With the committee structure in place, the next steps were to formulate and implement strategies to develop leadership skills and set the stage for individual leadership.

Leadership Development Strategies

We initiated three leadership development strategies at DBCC between September 1999 and May 2001. They were Presidential Leadership Seminars, the Beacon Leadership Program, and Situational Leadership Workshops. The three programs were designed to include a cross-section of college employees; representation from many different departments and divisions; and a diversity of ethnicity, culture, and experience. Key individuals currently in leadership roles, such as the president of the Faculty Senate and president of the Administrative Council, were included. Members of the President's Cabinet identified additional participants. Qualifications for participation were as follows:

- Potential to lead
- Commitment to the institution
- Openness to change

In addition to preparing new leaders, the program focused on facilitating change in institutional culture. Organizational culture is an important situational variable that influences all members of an organization. Because it is also a learned process, we believed it was logical to use formal leadership training to facilitate its change. Lawson and Shen (1998, 40) note that by teaching best practices to solve organizational problems, it is possible to change the actions, thoughts, and feelings of a large segment of members of the organization and thus change organizational culture.

Each of the three components of the program had a unique purpose and philosophy, and each has produced specific positive outcomes and lessons learned.

Presidential Leadership Seminars

The Presidential Leadership Seminars, DBCC's first formal leadership initiative, were launched in spring 2000. Twenty-one people were selected to participate in the first seminar, which lasted two and a half days. The presentations covered a wide range of topics related to leadership in higher education. Participants heard from current and former community college presidents and educational leaders. The speakers addressed the concept of leadership from every angle: from professional ethics to practical issues, from politics to priorities. The seminar was organized and facilitated by Jeff Hockaday, consultant and chancellor emeritus of Pima Community College. As DBCC president, I hosted the seminar; our vice presidents were present to provide input and feedback.

Three Presidential Leadership Seminars have now taken place, and 69 employees have participated. All sessions were held in a conference facility off campus. Each participant receives personalized materials, including an engraved pen and portfolio. College presidents and other individuals holding leadership roles in community colleges elsewhere in the state or the nation are invited as presenters. The cost for each seminar is about $25,000.

> In addition to preparing new leaders, the program focused on facilitating change in institutional culture.

Following each Leadership Seminar, we solicit feedback from members of the President's Cabinet as well as participants. They have hailed the seminars as an effective way to encourage employees to recognize and embrace the mantle of leadership.

The success of the seminars led to discussions about the need for a long-term formal program with a mentorship component, an idea that led to the Beacon Leadership Program.

Beacon Leadership Program

The concept of a collaborative leadership development program began to take shape in spring 2001. The 21st Century Educational Leadership Profile provided the foundation for additional formal leadership training and a structured mentorship program at DBCC. The Beacon Leadership Program began with two purposes in mind:
1. To incorporate educational theory, mentorship opportunities, and issue-focused problem-solving experiences into a formal leadership education program
2. To provide a mechanism through which the college's emerging leaders could earn graduate credit or advanced degrees

All alumni of the Presidential Leadership Seminars were eligible to apply to the Beacon Leadership Program. Additional persons were invited on the basis of recommendations from members of the President's Cabinet. Twenty-one participants enrolled in the first Beacon Leadership class. The college covered all expenses.

Classes were held on Friday evenings and Saturday mornings at DBCC for a six-week summer term. Participants were encouraged to relate their course work to their responsibilities at the college and to incorporate class assignments into their daily work activities whenever practicable.

The course focused on formal leadership theory as well as on practical leadership opportunities. Each participant was expected to engage in four activities:

1. Identification of critical issues at DBCC
2. Examination of the critical issues and formulation of recommendations
3. Presentation of the recommendations to the president and the President's Cabinet
4. Exploration of DBCC's institutional culture and decision-making processes

Participants who successfully completed the course received academic credits that were applicable toward a master's or doctoral degree through the University of Florida Educational Leadership, Policy, and Foundations Department. The team-oriented, problem-solving focus of the course resulted in four issue-related projects that are now in various stages of implementation at the college.

During the second semester, we incorporated a mentorship component into the Beacon Leadership Program. Each participant selected a mentor from the college's senior administration. The participant was to spend approximately 150 hours shadowing his or her mentor, discussing the mentor's work, and working on projects assigned by the mentor. The mentors were asked to share as much as possible with their mentees and to give them access to information that might normally not be shared.

Situational Leadership Workshops

The third component of the leadership program was a series of Situational Leadership Workshops. Attendees included individuals who had participated in previous leadership training or who had otherwise demonstrated leadership traits. Most of the Beacon Leadership Program participants were represented.

The workshops consisted of 10 case studies representing situations that had occurred at community colleges around the country. Names and other identifying information were omitted. A matrix was used to establish a team structure in which participants assumed the role of a community college president, vice president, or faculty member. In some cases, team members creatively changed their roles as they worked through the exercise. Each team was expected to formulate a solution to the case and present it to the group. The facilitator chose three participants to ask probing questions of the presenting team to ensure a critical discussion of the presentation.

The case studies provided an opportunity for participants to put into practice the ideas and concepts discussed during the previous leadership training events. The cost of each workshop was less than $5,000.

Recommendations of the Beacon Leadership Project Teams

Each Beacon Leadership Program participant was expected to complete an issue-focused project during the summer semester. The class was divided into four teams, each of which was assigned to research a real issue facing the college. The teams were to define the issues, research alternative strategies or solutions, analyze resources, and make recommendations for addressing the issues. Four areas were addressed:

1. Technology
2. Partnerships
3. Student retention
4. Communications

A summary of each project and its recommended action was presented to the President's Cabinet and the DBCC Board of Trustees. The projects are summarized below.

Technology

Following a review of the college's technology needs and an assessment of current and emerging technologies, the team recommended that DBCC use Internet portal technology to streamline student and administrative services.

A campus portal is an entry point on the Internet that provides a centralized source of information and services. A portal supports students, staff, alumni, faculty, and others by providing customized access to news, search functions, calendar and e-mail, class resources, and student activity. It offers numerous benefits related to student services, administrative services, and course capabilities. Development and implementation of a campus Internet portal would, the team believed, increase student retention and enhance external and internal communication.

The team analyzed expenses for three acquisition and implementation strategies: (1) build the portal internally; (2) partner with other colleges to build the portal; and

(3) acquire a portal through a commercial vendor. The optimal strategy for a college depends on the technical expertise of the information services department and the administrative software used for student systems.

Partnerships

To increase the college's effectiveness in developing and maintaining partnerships, this team recommended that DBCC reestablish its alumni association. By developing stronger ties and ongoing contact with former students and graduates, the team reasoned, the college could access a largely untapped resource and open doors to more effective partnerships.

The goal of the alumni association would be to enable the college to keep in touch with recent graduates and reconnect with earlier alumni in order to build stronger relationships with business and industry. DBCC graduates are an essential part of the regional workforce. Many employers are unaware of how many DBCC alumni they employ. If they realized the impact DBCC graduates had on their business, their willingness to support and be involved in the college would increase, the team suggested. The recommended focus was one of "friend raising" rather than "fundraising."

> A campus portal is an entry point on the Internet that provides a centralized source of information and services.

The team cited the following other potential benefits to the college:

- Increased partnership opportunities and more effective partnerships
- An improved image of the college within the community
- Establishment of grassroots advocacy alliances
- Increased business involvement in student mentoring, job shadowing, and tutoring

Student Retention

A four-year study revealed that less than 60 percent of Daytona Beach Community College students who start a degree or certificate program eventually graduate from DBCC. To improve the college's retention rate, this team recommended that DBCC implement a pilot mentoring program for at-risk students. The team reviewed the national literature related to community college retention, assessed current retention initiatives at the college, and interviewed members of a campuswide Retention Task

Force. With the concurrence of the task force, the team identified two target groups for a pilot mentoring program: students with undeclared majors and students in college preparatory classes.

The team's recommendation included staffing considerations, incentives for faculty involvement, and development of training materials. The team also estimated the cost of implementing and maintaining the program. Expected benefits of the program included increased and sustained enrollment and improved student success, as reflected in academic standing, graduation rates, and job placement.

Communications

As a result of an analysis of the literature, the communications team concluded that internal communications have been a key component of successful marketing strategies in the corporate world. Most experts concur that the future success of institutions of higher education will be driven by similar corporate approaches; nonetheless, some higher education institutions have not developed effective internal communications programs.

An assessment of the current situation at DBCC determined that improved processes implemented by the marketing department had strengthened the impact of the college's external marketing efforts. Similar improvements were needed for internal communications processes to ensure that key messages were consistently delivered.

The team recommended that the college formally evaluate its current internal communications process. With that information, an integrated communications model could be designed and implemented. Such a model would allow broad input from throughout the college, yet focus responsibility for internal communications in one area or department. Improved internal communications would, the team proposed, result in increased productivity, higher morale, and more effective teamwork.

Benefits of the Beacon Leadership Program

As Pfeffer (1977, 104) has noted, leadership is a system of relationships with constraints as well as opportunities. Leaders understand and are able to work within this system.

Observations of the Beacon participants revealed that they had acquired a new demeanor and a new sense of confidence. The participants were communicating the traits of leadership to those around them. They had learned that real leaders know that they are always communicating. The participants were skillfully, deliberately, and carefully making points and providing well-thought-out rationales for their proposed solutions. They were not only communicating the outcomes of their projects but also teaching others how to define a problem, analyze and research possible solutions, and develop a strong recommendation.

Lessons Learned

A review of the impact of the Beacon Leadership Program revealed the following important lessons:

- Given the appropriate opportunity, tools, and support, leaders can be developed.
- Not every person selected to participate in a leadership program will benefit from it; however, care should be taken not to judge anyone's potential during the selection process.
- When seeking potential leaders, it is beneficial to cast a wide net. Leaders are needed at all levels of the institution.
- Leadership skills already in the institution should be tapped to assist in the leadership development process. This practice not only provides needed assistance but also sends the right message to participants.
- Even leaders need applause. Give them plenty. Always recognize and acknowledge accomplishments.
- Planners should understand that it is all right to make mistakes. The purpose of leadership development is to develop leaders, not to achieve perfection.
- Leadership development should be a structured teaching and learning experience.

Participant Feedback

Beacon Leadership Program participants were surveyed midway through the program to gather feedback on the effectiveness of the program. A questionnaire was sent by e-mail to 24 Beacon participants; 16 responded. The questionnaire included four items:

1. On a scale of 1 to 10, rate your experience in the Beacon Leadership Program and provide some insight into your score.
2. What benefits have you realized personally, professionally, or organizationally as a result of your participation?

3. What challenges have you encountered during the program?
4. Please provide any additional comments you would like to make.

Participants noted that the program gave them a "new perspective on leadership" and a "broader understanding of the college." Many pointed out that they were experiencing a renewed enthusiasm for their roles as educators and leaders. Several of the respondents appreciated the mentorship as an opportunity to observe decision making at the highest level of the college and to compare and contrast different leadership styles.

When asked to identify any challenges they had encountered during the program, participants most often cited the time commitment. A majority of the respondents felt that the time involved made it difficult to maintain a balance between the Beacon classes and assignments, their job responsibilities, and their personal lives.

Some participants also expressed a need for clearer communication about the curriculum, schedule, and requirements for completing the graduate degree program. Some of these difficulties can be attributed to the long-distance nature of the program. While the Educational Leadership Department and faculty are accessible to Beacon participants, other departments involved in the program (e.g., the Admissions Department) are not.

Comments from Beacon Leadership Participants

The team building, sharing of ideas, and vast knowledge exchanged in this type of atmosphere are some of the best learning channels I have been associated with.

The Beacon program has allowed me to observe collegial teamwork. As professionals, we can agree to disagree and still work together.

I love the synergy and the opportunity it provides to work and learn from others of diverse backgrounds.

This experience is very satisfying because we are working on real issues that impact our own working environment while developing our leadership skills.

This program has helped me understand the organizational structure of the college. In so doing, it allows me to be supportive of the college's mission.

The opportunity to train to someday be part of the college's leadership team is very exciting for me. That we have decided to generate our future by looking at the human resources that exist within the institution creates an overall feeling of goodwill and should lead to a smooth transfer of leadership at the institution. I hope that more of my colleagues will have the opportunity to share in similar experiences.

Next Steps

Beacon Leadership participants who have completed all three parts of the leadership program have two options. The first option is to leave the program at the end of the year, by which time they will have earned 9 to 15 graduate credits and completed the 21st Century Educational Leadership Profile. The second is to apply to pursue a master's or doctoral degree in higher education administration from the University of Florida. Fifty percent of the original Beacon participants have elected to pursue advanced degrees. Upon becoming aware of the program, eight additional employees have requested to join the original cohort.

Conclusion

Development and training of leaders is a fundamental function of a learning organization (Lawson and Ventriss 1992, 205). To carry out its commitment to leadership development, DBCC will continue to provide opportunities to enhance skills, nurture talents, and seed ideas. The long-term impact of DBCC's leadership remains unknown; however, those who have participated in planning the program feel confident that programs such as this will have a positive effect on overcoming the impending leadership crisis facing community colleges.

References

Lawson, R. B., and Zheng Shen. 1998. *Organizational Psychology: Foundations and Applications.* New York: Oxford University Press.

Lawson, R. B., and C. L. Ventriss. 1992. "Organizational Change: The Role of Organizational Culture and Organizational Learning." *Psychological Record* 42: 205–219.

Lippman, W. 1945. *New York Herald Tribune*, 14 April.

Pfeffer, J. 1977. "The Ambiguity of Leadership." *Academy of Management Review* 2: 104–112.

PART II

LEADERSHIP

RECRUITMENT

AND SELECTION

CHAPTER 5

Recruiting and Developing Leaders for the 21st Century

Albert L. Lorenzo, President, and Daniel T. DeMarte,
Assistant to the President and Executive Director of Planning,
Macomb Community College

For more than a decade, authorities have been using words such as *transforma-tion, reengineering, restructuring, transition, reinvention,* and *renewal* to describe the extent to which they believe organizations will need to change if they are to thrive in the 21st century. Although the terminology may differ, there is almost unanimous accord that tomorrow's leaders must become adept at reshaping their organizations in fundamental ways. These strong and pervasive sentiments lead to two basic assumptions about the future of community colleges. First, to remain viable, community colleges must continue to change in significant ways. Second, the colleges' success will probably be determined by their ability to recruit and develop effective leaders.

This chapter begins with a discussion of how the principal functions of organizational leaders have evolved during the past century and how they are likely to change in the years ahead. It then describes in detail the three major strategies of a unique leadership development program used by Macomb Community College. Each may be called a "situational" strategy because it can be readily adapted to a specific institution's needs.

Leadership in the 20th Century

The nature of organizational leadership is constantly changing. As a result, efforts to recruit and develop leaders for the new century are best understood by positioning them on a continuum of change that began during the early part of the 20th century.

In the early 1900s, when management science was in its formative years, organizational leaders were advised to concentrate on the completion of tasks. The production-line concept of Henry Ford and the task analysis methods developed by Frederick Winslow Taylor exemplified this orientation. It was based on the idea that work should be broken down into manageable pieces and that the role of a leader (at that point, maybe best referred to as "manager") was to ensure that workers performed their designated tasks in an efficient and timely manner.

In pursuing this task-oriented approach, corporate planners showed far greater concern for finances, facilities, and equipment than they did for personnel. The result was an environment in which most of the employees were expected simply to "do," and only a select few were actually paid to "think."

By the midpoint of the last century, when automation began to redefine the nature of work, the effectiveness of this task-oriented approach was called into question. This was also the point at which the "doer-to-thinker" ratio began to shift. Later, as robots and chip technology came into use worldwide, it became apparent that a sustained competitive advantage would have to come from something other than capital investment alone. To be competitive, an organization would have to develop its human resources as well as its physical plant. Leaders began to complement their concern for the completion of tasks with a people-oriented approach. Human capital became a recognized resource.

Toward the end of the 20th century, a third dimension of effective leadership began to emerge. The environment within which most organizations were operating had become volatile and unpredictable. Time-tested strategies, products, and practices became obsolete quickly, and new approaches were continuously required. Leaders needed to become more adept at implementing organizational change. Some went so far as to suggest that the greatest challenge facing corporate leaders was not the management of change but the management of "surprise" (Schein 1993).

As we reflect on how the nature of leadership has evolved throughout the last century, we see evidence of three important characteristics: (1) an ever-present (but diminishing) emphasis on managing the completion of tasks; (2) a substantial commitment to developing human resources; and (3) an increasing emphasis on the ability to lead organizational change. These three characteristics are readily apparent in most of today's progressive organizations, including community colleges. (For those interested in greater detail, a study by Leslie and Velsor [1996] provides insight into individual "success and derailment factors" within task-, people-, and change-oriented leadership contexts.)

Leadership for the New Century

Those three characteristics will likely remain central to effective leadership in the years ahead. At the same time, three additional factors will quickly find their way into the leadership equation. They are (1) the decentralization of leadership authority, (2) an emphasis on conflict resolution, and (3) the facilitation of individual and organizational learning.

On the basis of current trends, we may conclude that leadership will become more pluralistic. Organizations are entering what might be called the "post-heroic age" of leadership—an age in which it will no longer be possible, or even desirable, for one individual at the top to be the single driving force behind an enterprise. A single leader may be essential during an organization's formative years, but as that organization evolves, leadership teams will likely emerge. In fact, "teams" and the "decentralization of leadership authority" are recurring themes in some of the late-20th-century literature on high-performing systems.

For example, in applying the lessons he learned from studying 46 major corporations to higher education, Wilson (1994) states that individuals at the top of an organization should no longer be expected to do everything. He believes that the real planners must be the line managers, not the staff planners or senior officers. Schein (1993) underscores the psychological value of teams. He suggests that the anxieties inherent in this new age of leadership will be tolerable only if they are shared by a group that is accountable for the organization's welfare. For these and other equally valid reasons, the ability to develop effective teams will probably become a prerequisite to institutional leadership.

Moreover, as time passes, a greater proportion of leadership energy will be devoted to resolving conflicts and clarifying values. Munitz (1995), for instance, argues that higher education leaders will need a new set of tools. "Rather than placating constituencies," he says, these leaders are being called upon to "use conflict constructively" (14). Likewise, in a survey of more than 500 college and university presidents, Stanton and Pitsvada (1993) found that three of the five top focus areas of emerging leadership were resolving conflict, promoting collaboration, and ensuring equity.

Finally, future leaders will be called upon to facilitate both individual and organizational learning. Senge (1990), who popularized the concept of the "learning organization," argues that learning disabilities are fatal in organizations. He believes that leaders must build an environment where people continually expand their capacity to create the results they truly desire and where they can learn together. Kim (1993) observes that all organizations learn, whether they consciously choose to or not, because it is a fundamental requirement for their continued existence. He sees a critical link between individual and organizational learning, noting that "organizations ultimately learn via their individual members" (37). Colleges, therefore, should find a way to link ongoing professional development with their leadership development programs.

In summary, leaders of this century will increasingly be asked to share authority by working in teams, to resolve conflicts by clarifying values, and to make a commitment to continuous learning through professional development.

Three Situational Leadership Development Strategies

The 2001 American Association of Community Colleges (AACC) Leadership Survey (Shults 2001) revealed that 45 percent of current community college presidents plan to retire within the next six years and that an additional 34 percent will be retiring within seven to 10 years. The outlook is similar for faculty and other chief administrative officers. In an unpublished white paper written for the AACC, Katsinas and Kempner (2001) refer to the situation as a "crisis of leadership development." The future success of community colleges clearly will be influenced by their ability to recruit and develop leaders.

> Although most colleges are facing the same challenge, it may not be wise for them to employ the same strategies.

Although most colleges are facing the same challenge, it may not be wise for them to employ the same strategies. As community-based institutions, community colleges are intended to respond to local needs and conditions. By design, these colleges mirror the communities that created them. Not too long ago, the United States was a fairly monolithic nation, and colleges could easily use one another's programs and services. During the past two decades, communities have become increasingly dissimilar—demographically, economically, politically, and culturally. As this trend continues, institutions will be less and less able to use someone else's answers. They will need strategies tailored to meet the specific situations on their campuses.

The three programs described in this chapter were selected as examples of effective leadership development strategies because they can easily be adapted to differing situations. The first strategy, the Janus Program, is a leadership recruitment initiative that can be tailored to the specific needs of an institution. The second strategy involves the Institute of Higher Education (IHE) 21st Century Educational Leadership Profile. Both have been piloted at Macomb Community College over the past three years. The third program is a new performance-appraisal process— Achieving Collective Effectiveness (ACE)—about to be piloted. It is intended to more closely align individual efforts with organizational goals and to foster professional development experiences that will lead to improved individual and team performance.

The Janus Program: Recruiting When Leaders Are Ready

Driven by an anticipated 50 percent turnover in its leadership ranks, Macomb developed the Janus Program in 1998 as a means of recruiting future leaders as they become ready to assume such responsibility, rather than as posts become vacant. The name *Janus* was taken from that of the Greek god who looked forward and backward at the same time. It is symbolic of the program's attempt to honor the contributions of outgoing leaders and, at the same time, welcome and celebrate new leaders.

Each Janus position has four elements: (1) a program objective; (2) a description of the position; (3) targeted candidates; and (4) a program structure and implementation. Its unique feature is a "continuous vacancy," triggered by the nomination of a candidate for a position rather than by the departure of an incumbent leader. The number of Janus positions may vary by institutional size and need; Macomb has budgeted funds to support up to three full-time positions at any one time.

The objective of the Janus Program is to provide a beneficial experience not only for the aspiring administrators who are selected to participate in the program but also for the college. Participants gain valuable work experience that prepares them for permanent employment at Macomb or, if necessary, at another college. The college provides mentoring for the candidates. In turn, it has an opportunity to advance its mission, to ensure the accomplishment of important administrative duties and responsibilities, to develop new strategic alliances, and to energize the administrative ranks.

The position title given to Janus Program participants is project development administrator (PDA). A new PDA is typically assigned to the college's planning unit for a six- to nine-month orientation. During this time, he or she becomes acclimated to the college culture while working on assigned projects. Following the orientation, participants may be assigned to other units within the college. They must be willing to be assigned to a variety of projects and to blend the needs of the college with their personal career interests. This strategy allows participants an opportunity to gain a wide range of experiences and to identify a career niche.

Candidates must have, or be quite near to receipt of, an earned doctorate degree from a program with a national reputation for excellence in community college leadership. Every candidate must be nominated by a nationally recognized faculty member from an aforementioned program or by an association executive with a similar national reputation for involvement in a leadership development program. Candidates are asked to make a commitment of one to three years to the college. Typical candidates have no more than three years' work experience in higher education administration and have research experience. They are knowledgeable of quantitative and qualitative research methodologies and aware of current issues in higher education. They are treated as full-time administrators in terms of professional responsibilities, performance assessment, salary and benefits, and membership in the collective-bargaining unit.

The Janus Program enables the college to fill vacant positions more quickly and with greater flexibility than it could using a traditional hiring process. Using traditional methods, triggered by the departure of an incumbent administrator, the college took from 10 weeks to six months to fill a position. The hiring process under the Janus Program is triggered by nominations to the college president. Approval of nominees requires no more than four weeks.

Macomb had traditionally created a separate committee to review and screen applicants for each vacancy; however, under Janus, a standing review panel is responsible for program oversight. The review panel comprises four or five persons, including the president, a vice president, a collective bargaining appointee, and the director of planning. In cases in which the candidate has a specific career interest, a fifth administrator from that area may be added to the panel. The panel is responsible for the general oversight of the program including (1) reviewing background, experience, and general fit of participants to the college and the position; (2) interviewing potential participants; (3) reviewing, creating, and prioritizing projects or strategic initiatives for the applicant; (4) assigning participants to projects or strategic initiatives, units, and mentors; (5) conducting performance evaluations on candidates at the end of each assignment; (6) assessing the effectiveness of the program (e.g., reviewing appropriateness of assigned projects and ensuring that mentoring occurs); and (7) preparing a recommendation for the president regarding long-term employment. Each panel member serves for three years.

The Janus Program has been under way since 1998. Lessons learned to date include the following:

- The program must be perceived as a credible way to identify and hire talented individuals.

- Mentoring must be taken seriously, and it is time-consuming. Therefore, the program should be limited to three or four participants at a time.

- Some candidates have had direct experience and an educational background well beyond what would normally be required for an entry-level position, so such a position may not be attractive to them.

- The program has strengthened the college's strategic alliances with doctoral programs preparing community college leaders and with national associations providing services to community colleges.

The Leadership Profile: A Road Map for Individual and Team Development

Almost every college provides some form of professional development opportunities for its staff. These opportunities generally include paying for subscriptions to professional publications, for association memberships, and for conference attendance, as well as sponsoring on-campus presentations on topics of interest. Though effective in many ways, this traditional approach is rarely useful for identifying and developing specific attributes within an individual.

In 1998, Macomb Community College was invited to become one of a dozen institutions to pilot test the 21st Century Educational Leadership Profile launched at the IHE. Macomb's principal interest was to use this tool to strengthen its senior leadership team and to customize professional development plans for individual members of the team. So far, the results have been highly satisfactory.

The most immediate benefit to the college was gaining access to the Leadership Profile itself. This compilation of 20 work-related attributes, classified as Essential, Important, or Other Relevant, provided a road map for individualized development plans and became the learning outcomes for our professional development and team-building experiences.

The president was the first to use the Leadership Profile, followed by members of the President's Council. About six months later, administrators at the next reporting level were given the opportunity to participate. No one was required to participate, but so far all but one of the leaders invited to use the Leadership Profile have accepted. (The person who declined did so because he was about to retire.)

The most noteworthy and consistent feedback from participants in the project has been how accurately the Occupational Personality Questionnaire (OPQ) assessed their preferred work styles. Many senior administrators had participated in similar style assessments earlier in their careers, but none had agreed so fully with the results of these earlier surveys as they had with those of the OPQ. Each participant received a Person–Job Match Report that compared his or her assessed abilities, skills, and personality attributes against attributes ranked as Essential, Important, and Other Relevant.

The college developed a composite of the President's Council members' profiles. This composite charted individual scores in eight key aspects of leadership and team contribution: Coordinator, Shaper, Innovator, Monitor/Evaluator, Resource Investigator, Completer, Team Worker, and Implementer (Figure 5.1).

While there was a fair amount of consistency among team members, some differences did exist. The differences were healthy, because they enabled team members to appropriately challenge the ideas and directions of the group. As Figure 5.1 shows, Macomb's team members consistently scored highest on Coordinator and Implementer, although the widest range of scores was in the latter category.

The college decided to use the results of the OPQ as part of a self-directed professional development program. Each participant was given his or her completed report; the president's office kept only the cover letter and a one-page profile graph.

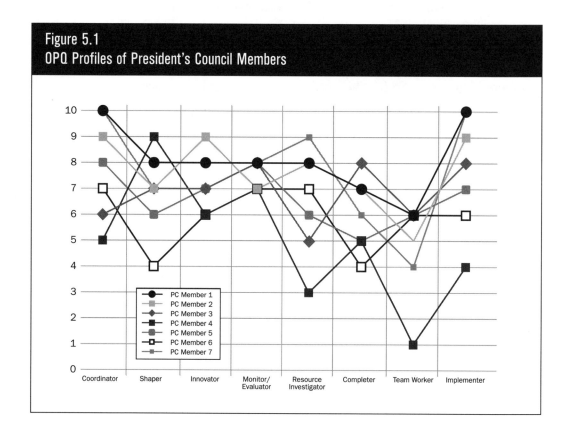

Figure 5.1
OPQ Profiles of President's Council Members

Participants were asked to review their report in detail, share or discuss it with colleagues and their supervisors, and identify activities and experiences that would strengthen specific elements of their leadership abilities. By design, the college made no formal record of individual progress, and none of the results were used for evaluative purposes. Participation in the program was presented and reinforced as an opportunity, not a requirement.

The participants have used the match report and related professional development experiences to varying degrees. Some have moved into more responsible roles, but because the participants already held senior positions, most have remained in the same jobs. The leadership team has learned more about itself as a team, and all participants

> **Participation in the program was presented and reinforced as an opportunity, not a requirement.**

have experienced some benefit, even if it was no more than an opportunity to take a long look at their reflection in a very accurate leadership mirror. Macomb plans to continue using the Leadership Profile and the OPQ with new staff and will most likely offer the opportunity to aspiring leaders as they are identified.

ACE: Aligning Performance with Purpose

As Macomb finds gaps in team and individual profiles, it plans to use a new performance management system—Achieving Collective Effectiveness (ACE)—to focus on areas for growth and development and thereby better align individual and team performance with broad organizational purposes and strategies.

ACE is a process, not an event. It encourages team building, individual excellence, and organizational effectiveness as functions of the performance appraisal process. It focuses on desired results, and it integrates individual achievement with college effectiveness by identifying and cultivating key values and behaviors. Establishing clear performance expectations is an important part of the system. These expectations come from two areas: (1) alignment of strategic organizational goals to the individual; and (2) identification of behavioral expectations based on organizational values.

The following themes are recognized as fundamental elements of the ACE system:

■ Involve staff in the development of an appraisal system. Ownership and commitment from everyone involved are critical to the success of performance management. When staff members feel engaged in the future of the organization, attributes such as ownership, pride, and enthusiasm begin to develop.

- Define performance expectations. Make sure that performance expectations, in terms of desired behavior and goal accomplishment, are clearly stated and mutually understood. When expectations are agreed upon, an employee's performance becomes more focused.

- Value human resources in organizational effectiveness. Organizations grow as their people do. As staff members internalize the vision of the organization, institutional effectiveness becomes a shared goal.

- Develop a supportive organizational culture. Conducting performance appraisals is more about cultivating a desired culture than it is about conducting personnel evaluations. For performance management to work, it must be conducted in an environment characterized by shared values, open communication, and modeled behaviors.

- Provide professional development. Professional development should be closely aligned with performance management. Both individual and organizational effectiveness are contingent on proper training and on development of leadership and technical skills.

- Make appraisals an ongoing process. Performance management should be based on a philosophy of continuous improvement. It should be integrated in all aspects of the organization's development.

Summary

Expectations of educational leaders will continue to grow, while the supply of highly effective leaders will continue to shrink. This means that colleges must become proactive in their quest for leaders.

Using the Janus Program, the 21st Century Educational Leadership Profile, and the ACE performance management system, Macomb Community College has taken a significant step toward addressing the leadership challenge. The college has formed a useful profile of the attributes it is seeking in its future leaders, and it has put in place a process that enables the college to fill vacancies more efficiently. Macomb has also found a reliable instrument to help design individualized professional development plans for current and future administrators, as well as a means to reinforce development objectives through a newly designed appraisal process. Taken collectively, these actions have made positive differences in the college's leadership teams and individual performance.

Each institution must form its own strategies that respond to and reflect its unique context. What works at one college may not work at another. Nonetheless, the initiatives undertaken at Macomb might be investigated by other institutions, even to provide a point of departure for other leadership recruitment and development efforts.

> As staff members internalize the vision of the organization, institutional effectiveness becomes a shared goal.

References

Katsinas, Stephen G., and Ken Kempner. March 2001. "The Crisis of Leadership Development for Community Colleges: A Policy Imperative." Unpublished white paper prepared for the American Association of Community Colleges, Washington, D.C.

Kim, D. 1993. "The Link between Individual and Organizational Learning." *Sloan Management Review* 35 (1): 37–50.

Leslie, J., and E. Velsor. 1996. *A Look at Derailment Today: North America and Europe.* Greensboro, N.C.: The Center for Creative Leadership.

Munitz, B. 1995. "Wanted: New Leadership for Higher Education." *Planning for Higher Education* 24 (9): 9–16.

Schein, E. 1993. "How Can Organizations Learn Faster? The Challenge of Entering the Green Room." *Sloan Management Review* 34(2): 85–92.

Senge, Peter M. 1990. *The Fifth Discipline: The Art and Practice of the Learning Organization.* New York: Doubleday.

Shults, Christopher. 2001. *The Critical Impact of Impending Retirements on Community College Leadership.* Research Brief Leadership Series, no. 1, AACC-RB-01-5. Washington, D.C.: American Association of Community Colleges.

Stanton, T., and B. Pitsvada. 1993. "Emerging Presidential Styles." *College and University* 68(1): 12–21.

Wilson, I. 1994. "The Strategic Management of Higher Education: Lessons from Corporate Experience." *On the Horizon* 2(3): 1–3.

CHAPTER 6

Reaching Diverse Populations and Using New Tools in Executive Selection

Frank William Reis, Executive Vice President, Human Resources and Administration, Cuyahoga Community College

As customer-focused businesses, community colleges require top performers on staff. They need people who can establish and maintain relationships with people, solve problems, and take a positive approach to life and work. Simply put, any search for new personnel is an exercise in public relations and an opportunity to improve the college's image within the community as a whole (Higgins and Hollander 1987, 1). Organizations that identify talent on the basis of the candidate's natural abilities, as well as his or her learned skills, often experience measurable improvements in such areas as customer satisfaction and staff turnover (Wreed 1999). Equally important, community colleges today need to be aware of maintaining staff diversity in gender, ethnicity, and age.

These observations hold particularly true in the recruitment of a college's executive leadership team—the most visible representation of an institution's employee base and hiring strategy. A community college's leadership team must reflect all interests of a dynamic work environment as well as the needs of the community it serves. A consideration of diversity, teamed with a firm knowledge of the proper qualifications and skills for any open position, is key to a successful recruitment process. A variety of tools can help community colleges achieve this goal.

Proper Tools Streamline the Search Process and Reduce Turnover

Traditional employee recruitment techniques, while still effective and used in nearly every candidate search, are now often complemented by new, targeted approaches that single out qualified candidates on all levels of the hiring spectrum. Every successful executive recruitment strategy requires internal and external tools that will enable an organization to find the right leader for the position. Used correctly, these tools can help institutions create a tailor-made hiring match.

Cuyahoga Community College (Tri-C) is a multicampus, single-college, comprehensive educational institution with a diverse student body of more than 21,000 credit students and a full- and part-time workforce of more than 2,800. Approximately 32 percent of our student body are members of minority groups. We have the largest number of African American and Hispanic American students of all of Ohio's postsecondary schools. The Tri-C workforce mirrors the diversity of the student body and the community; about 31 percent of faculty, staff, and administrative employees are members of a minority group. The executive team of the college embodies the college's claim that "Diversity is our strength." Five of the nine members of the executive team are women and four of those nine are members of minority groups.

Building and sustaining a strong, diverse executive team is an ongoing challenge for Tri-C. Our executive recruitment process must assess an individual's ability to fit the college's culture. We also must put in place effective hiring practices and tools that allow them to make timely hiring decisions.

Employee turnover is less than 7 percent per year. This percentage is not high, given that many faculty and staff members within community colleges are approaching retirement age or have accumulated the number of years of service needed to retire, or both. Still, identifying and hiring qualified leaders is an ongoing concern.

What must a college do to attract and retain a diverse workforce? The challenge requires creative thinking about recruiting and recruiting resources. Also, a college must ensure that candidates are attracted to the college's mission, its environment for learning and working, and its commitment to diversity.

Quality-of-Life Issues Play Role in Attracting Candidates

For the past decade, Tri-C has focused on quality-of-life initiatives for employees and a desire to make a difference in the lives of our students. Quality of life includes providing a healthy, safe, and learning environment for all. We sponsor an annual, collegewide Diversity Day, and we hold a Partnership through Diversity Series, which consists of lectures and other forms of cultural events for students, faculty, staff, and the community. A Show Time at High Noon Series showcases international cultural events. We strive to create an exemplary learning and working environment for all.

We realize that to achieve this goal we must recruit quality faculty members, staff, and administrators. The following sections describe some of the lessons that Tri-C has learned as a result of its leadership recruitment efforts.

Tried-and-True Methods Are No Longer the Best

In the pre-Internet days, recruitment was simple. If you wanted to limit a search to local candidates, you placed a classified advertisement in a local newspaper. If you wanted to tap a national applicant base, you would place an advertisement in the *New York Times* or another large newspaper and in trade publications. You would post the opening on employee bulletin boards and in the human resources newsletter (McCarter and Schreyer 1999). You would then wait for the applications to arrive in the mail.

These techniques still have an important function because they reach a wide audience of candidates. Tri-C's staffing team, however, now supplements these strategies with other internal and external tools and networks that connect Tri-C with the qualified candidates for employment.

Reexamine and Fine-Tune Your Recruitment Strategy

For many years, Tri-C had a traditional employment structure led by a director of staffing and carried out by staff employment specialists. The process was unduly bureaucratic, and the time required to fill positions was much longer than it should have been. Positions often had to be reposted. We were not moving quickly enough in an increasingly competitive environment.

To overcome some of these challenges, we created a client-based service delivery model. Specific recruiters from the employment office were assigned to specific units, offices, and disciplines across the college. This model allowed recruiters to build closer relationships with the areas to which they had been assigned and to understand the competencies required to fill positions within their assigned client group. This client-based structure appears to be working well.

Internal Sources and Networks Provide Excellent Leads

Over the years, employee networks have assisted in creating diverse and inclusive cultures within the American workplace, whether it is corporate, governmental, or academic. These networks, also known as business resources, caucuses, or affinity groups, help provide outreach to diverse communities, shape human resources politics, and develop business strategy (Brotherton 2000). Tri-C's diverse employment base provides an excellent internal network for locating qualified candidates from an equally diverse population. The three major components of this network are the Black Caucus, the Hispanic Steering Council, and the Governance Advisory Committee on Human Resources and Policy. The Black Caucus and the Hispanic Steering Council work directly with administrators in the college's human resources department and its administration. The college's Governance Advisory Committee works directly with the executive level within the Office of Academic and Student Affairs.

The Black Caucus has particular interest in the recruitment and retention of African American employees throughout the college. The caucus assists human resources staff on issues of recruitment, retention, and hiring in order to help ensure that diversity in the classroom is reflected within the ranks of faculty and staff. It helps identify sites, associations, and other resources that are then integrated into the college's recruitment plans for that year.

Created in 1992, the Hispanic Steering Council identifies, prioritizes, develops, and implements Hispanic initiatives that benefit both the college and the Cleveland Hispanic community. The council serves as an advisory committee to Tri-C administrators on Hispanic issues and as a liaison between the college and the local Hispanic population. It identifies and facilitates initiatives to promote the recruitment and retention of Hispanics at Tri-C. It has provided the staffing and recruitment team with resources to be used for attracting Hispanic candidates for employment opportunities at the college. These resources include local Hispanic social service and educational agencies, Spanish-language newspapers, and national publications. Additionally, the council provides support by distributing information through its own postal and e-mail lists and by posting and reading messages on a Cleveland Latino e-mail list.

The Governance Advisory Committee on Human Resources and Policy reviews and recommends policies and procedures related to rights and responsibilities, affirmative action, and due process. It addresses such issues as recruitment and outreach and provides the college with input regarding future directions. Several years ago, this committee helped identify more than 100 new locations where notices of administrative and faculty positions could be posted.

Human resources staff also use staff and faculty biographies to create an internal recruiting information network. These biographies provide information on each employee's membership in professional, social, and civic organizations and allow the staffing team to identify networking opportunities at an employee level.

Figure 6.1 is a sample list of outreach contacts routinely used by Tri-C in recruitment efforts. All job postings are sent to these sources. The list is periodically revised.

**Figure 6.1
Sample of Tri-C's Outreach Contacts**

- Cleveland American Indian Center
- City of Cleveland
  - Personnel Office
  - Community Cultural Affairs
  - Community Relations Board
- National Association for the Advancement of Colored People
- Jewish Vocational Services
- Catholic Counseling Center
- Vocational Guidance Services
- John Carroll University Office of Multi-Cultural Affairs
- Cleveland State University
  - Affirmative Action Office
  - Career Services Center
- Ohio Civil Rights Commission
- Ohio Bureau of Employment
- Urban League of Greater Cleveland
- Cleveland Council of Black College Alumni
- Veterans Administration
- Youth Opportunities Unlimited
- Catholic Charities Services
- Senior Community Services Employment
- Council for Economic Opportunities
- Women's Center of Greater Cleveland
- West Side Ecumenical Ministry
- Ohio Hispanic Social Services Workers Association
- Legal Aid Society
- Ohio City Near West Development Corporation
- City of Cleveland—Cleveland State University—Multicultural Program and Minority Affairs
- Center for Families and Children
- Employment and Training Council
- Central State University
- Parma Adult Training Center
- Goodwill Industries

Internet Recruiting

The college's staffing and recruitment team uses nearly 50 Internet recruiting sites to post job openings and recruit candidates (see sidebar). Internet recruiting has many advantages. It is much less expensive than many other means and allows access to a broad pool of candidates. Subscribers pay a fee; prospective employees often can access job postings at no cost. Some sites are general; others specialize. Macomb has used Internet sites to recruit all levels and types of professional staff positions.

Electronic Applicant Management Provides Quick Access to Candidates

The college enters application information from prospective employees into Resumix™, an electronic tracking system. Resumix™ assists the staffing team in narrowing the applications by applying image processing, knowledge-based software, and database technologies. It permits the team to catalog each applicant's resume and data and to create a profile of that person. This profile can be accessed online and printed at the request of a hiring committee member. It reduces paperwork and provides a way to keep track of applicants and their qualifications.

Systems such as this one will be critical for the future. The key to efficient recruitment and hiring is to reduce duplication of effort and reduce the time required to recruit and hire. Traditional methods of filling positions are no longer adequate. Institutions that are nimble, resilient, and focused will be able to move quickly in hiring the right leader in the timeliest way possible.

Profile Facilitates Analysis of Short-List Finalists

Tri-C has recently begun to use the 21st Century Educational Leadership Profile and the Occupational Personality Questionnaire (OPQ). Evaluating a candidate's talent using methods such as the Leadership Profile enables the hiring team not only to select the right people objectively but also to understand where in the organization the person would best fit.

The college used the Leadership Profile in 2000, when it was in the final stage of interviewing for a president for one of its three campuses. Before these interviews, the final four candidates took the OPQ. On the basis of the profile's information, the interview team framed questions that granted us deeper insight into the candidate's overall leadership style and core competencies. The college feels confident that this process assisted in hiring the right person.

■ **www.aacc.nche.edu.** This Web site of the American Association of Community Colleges allows national and international searches for positions that range from president to intern. Users can search for positions using filters such as salary, geography, education level, travel requirements, and key words. Professional development opportunities are also listed, and the site's variety of resources allows users to quickly access additional information about potential employers.

■ **CCollegejobs.com.** Subscribers may post an unlimited number of vacancies. The screening technology allows users to "mine" the resume database and target specific qualifications. Job seekers can post resumes and access postings at no cost. The site is related to the Kaleidoscope Leadership Institute for women of color educators, an institute that assists participants to prepare for and gain leadership positions in higher education and helps current leaders gain a greater understanding of ethnic differences and similarities.

■ **DiversityInc.com.** The career center at this site is a valuable recruitment tool for institutions that value diversity. Users must register before they can post resumes or use the job-searching tools. These applicants want to work for "diversity enthusiasts," and they are generally a highly skilled group of prospective employees.

■ **ccJobsOnline.** This site is presented by GetaJob, Inc., and *Community College Week.* This Internet source also targets outreach within the community college ranks.

■ **Flipdog.com.** This site is especially strong for technology-based occupations. It is free of charge to job seekers. For employers, it is less costly than and equally effective as similar sites with a national scope.

■ **StaffingMaster.com.** This local Cleveland-focused site enables employers to post a vacancy on up to 1,500 Internet job sites.

■ **Higheredjobs.com.** This site provides job seekers with several search options to help them narrow their options. Tri-C has an institutional profile listed on this site, as well as links to the college's home page and its human resources home page and to sites about Cleveland and the surrounding area.

■ **CareerBoard.com.** The site offers subscribers the ability to post an unlimited number of jobs, to create a company profile page, and to gain access to a resume database. Job seekers can post resumes and access job postings free of charge.

■ **Monster.com** and **HotJobs.com.** These sites are general sources that provide an excellent means of reaching job seekers.

Summary

By using tools such as electronic recruitment and the Leadership Profile, Tri-C has expanded its reach within the workforce. We have increased our ability to recruit from a diverse base of people, simplified our recruitment methods, improved the way we screen applicant information, and, most important, increased the likelihood that we will identify the right person for the job.

We realize that we must use a range of tools that reach audiences in all manners, from traditional newspaper advertising to the Internet, from internal networks to involvement with contacts in the local community and beyond.

While the methods described in this chapter work for us, we also recognize that different types of positions require different combinations of recruiting tools and strategies in order to be successful. It takes a combination of ingenuity, determination, and flexibility to develop a hiring strategy that delivers excellent results.

References

Brotherton, Phaedra. 2000. "Employee Networks Help Advance Diversity Efforts." Mosaics™ Newsletter. Society for Human Resource Management (July/August): 1.

Cuyahoga Community College. 2000. Executive Summary: "Student Success, Where Futures Begin."

Higgins, John M., and Patricia Hollander. 1987. *A Guide to Successful Searches for College Personnel: Policies, Procedures, and Legal Issues.* Asheville, N.C.: College Administration Publications.

McCarter, John, and Ray Schreyer. 1999. "Get Moving on the Recruiting Super-highway." *HRFOCUS American Management Association Conference Daily* (April): 76 (4).

Shults, Christopher. 2001. *The Critical Impact of Impending Retirements on Community College Leadership.* Research Brief Leadership Series, no. 1, AACC-RB-01-5. Washington, D.C.: American Association of Community Colleges.

Wreed, Katie. 1999. "Identifying Natural Talents Lets Company Make Right Choice." *HRFOCUS American Management Association Conference Daily* (April): 6.

CHAPTER 7

Selecting Community College Presidents for the 21st Century: A Trustee's Perspective

Carol Nasworthy, Trustee, Austin Community College

hoosing the person with whom to entrust the future of a college is a daunting task. The president is responsible for the success of students, the morale of faculty, the fiscal stability of the college, and compliance with accreditation standards. Selecting a new president may be the most important job a board of trustees has. Any trustee embarking on the task, particularly for the first time, may be overwhelmed by the importance of the decision. Trustees at Austin Community College (ACC), Texas, conducted two presidential searches within a few years, an experience that serves as the basis for the lessons shared in this chapter.

A successful college president needs a combination of many qualities—an understanding of what education is really about, some capacity for administration (which includes the ability to deal with people), a high degree of physical and emotional stamina, honesty, courage, personal integrity, and leadership skills.

No single person can be expected to possess all these qualities; thus, the search for an ideal candidate seems doomed to failure. Trustees at ACC learned this fact during our most recent presidential search in 1997. After receiving public input in open hearings at each of the seven ACC campuses and conducting focus groups with stakeholder groups comprising students, faculty, business organizations, and others, the Presidential Search Committee developed a candidate profile—a list of personal qualities, professional skills, and relevant experience we expected to find in our ideal candidate. Earl Maxwell, the cochair of the committee, noted the complexity of the task in a letter he sent to the committee:

> *[It is] clear from questions asked by the Advisory Committee that we are searching for a president who can perform almost superhuman feats...to work effectively with the Board (of Trustees) and be the spokesman for the college in*

various external forums (raise funds from the business community, establish strategic alliances with various organizations, participate in multicultural disputes, communicate with area universities, participate in civic associations and monitor environmental issues, among others). Also we expect the president to solve a host of internal problems (ranging from improving employee morale to solving budget and accreditation issues), while learning people's names (including the students')!

Presumably, the ideal candidate would also be able to "outrace locomotives and leap tall buildings in a single bound."

As our search continued, we soon learned that compromise would be essential. What follows are lessons learned, offered from one veteran trustee's perspective, in the hope that her experience and observations will be helpful to other trustees beginning this most important task.

The Context of Each Search Is Unique

As John W. Nason (1988, 118) points out in the *Handbook of College and University Trusteeship*, there is no such thing as a model college president. "The individual who might put on a brilliant performance at one institution," says Nason, "could easily be a dismal failure at another. Before deciding whom they want, trustees must decide what they want."

Trustees should start with a hardheaded analysis of the institution's problems and prospects. From the analysis, leaders can deduce the particular skills and qualifications most important for this president at this time, whether academic leadership ability, political savvy, fundraising ability, managerial skills, fiscal competence, public relations skills, or the ability to act as a conciliator. No one is equally good in all departments; for any college looking for a new president, some skills or abilities will be more important than others.

Whether the vacancy results from retirement, perhaps following a lengthy tenure, or from a president's sudden and unexpected exit, the machinery of selection is similar. However, contextual factors such as economic climate, academic offerings, and public opinion—which are constantly evolving—are central to the decision of the "best" person to lead the institution at a given moment. Therefore, trustees must do an environmental scan before launching a search.

The things that go into making an effective leader are many, elusive and varied. One of the intangible ingredients in the leadership formula is what some people refer to as chemistry or "fit." The fit may be right when a president first assumes a position but may later become so incompatible as to make the situation unbearable. Why? Circumstances change; presidents change; faculties change; administrators change; and most importantly boards change, especially in community colleges. Board members who employ a president have a vested interest in the president they hire; subsequent board members have less of a vested interest in that particular president. (Vaughan 1990, 5)

The importance of the environment is illustrated dramatically by ACC's experience. In 1993, ACC launched a search for a new president to replace an individual who had served in the post for 16 years. The college environment at that time was relatively stable, characterized by low administrative turnover, acceptable academic accreditation, general employee satisfaction, a history of balanced budgets, and a positive public image. A second search, conducted in 1997, took place in a significantly different environment. The board and the college at that time had a negative public image that had resulted from the short tenure of the departing president, a projected budget deficit, and a warning from Southern Association of College Standards that the college was in danger of losing accreditation. Several long-time administrators had retired or resigned to take other jobs, creating the perception of a loss of strength at the top level of the organization. The local Chamber of Commerce and business community were demanding that the college's program, which had traditionally emphasized academic transfer, be expanded to address current workforce training needs. Clearly, the contextual environments of the searches mandated particular, and different, skills and experience in the presidential candidates.

> Trustees must do an environmental scan before launching a search.

Make the News Media Your Friend

Not long before ACC's second search, the local public school district had begun to search for a new superintendent of schools. The school board announced that the search was confidential and refused to divulge any details of the process they were using or the names of any candidates for the position. The news media, particularly the daily newspaper, challenged the board's decision and filed suit against the school district under the Texas Open Records laws. As the lawsuit wound its way through the courts, the school board refused to give an inch. Daily front-page news stories and editorials criticized the school board's process and inflamed the public.

Reporters began to use aggressive investigative strategies to identify candidates and publish their names and backgrounds. This atmosphere had a chilling effect on the search.

The first ACC search had been conducted with little public attention, but given the changed environment, it was clear the second search might be a topic of greater media scrutiny. The board decided to make the media a friend. The cochairs of the Search Committee visited the editorial board of the town's major newspaper, the editors of all local newspapers, and the news directors of local radio and TV outlets. The ACC visitors explained that full disclosure about candidates would hamper the search process, because many candidates would not want their names to be divulged until they knew they were considered serious candidates for the position. The college pledged to fully inform the media about the progress of the search and invited reporters to attend all meetings of the advisory committee. The media agreed not to identify any specific candidates until finalists were selected.

This collaborative approach resulted in media coverage that was informative and factual rather than suspicious and investigative. Moreover, media coverage of campus events in general became more frequent, more comprehensive, and more accurate.

Professional Search Consultants Can Be Invaluable

The use of professional consultants is often a controversial matter. Resistance to the use of professional search consultants is often based on the conviction that trustees, faculty, and students understand the character and needs of the institution better than any outsider could. Cost, which often seems high to trustees, is also a concern. Further, many trustees do not understand the amount of time necessary for each stage of the search and selection process. At one time it may have been a simple, straightforward task, but that is not true today. As Beatrice Doser (1991, 8), a trustee at Montcalm Community College in Sidney, Michigan, has noted, "It can take up to two years. During this period there may be a reevaluation of college priorities. Then an elaborate and rather expensive search procedure commences involving the entire college and part of the community. It absorbs the energies of many people for many months."

By the time a search is completed, a new president is hired, and the college has stabilized, one to two years may have elapsed. If the new president does not work out, the process must be repeated, and the college may find itself on a downhill slide that will be hard to stop. Many boards now consider use of a consultant as an investment that saves time and money in the long run and also provides assurance that the search will be efficient, effective, and legal.

Approximately 20 percent of colleges and universities looking for new presidents use outside consultants to help define institutional needs and presidential criteria or to develop a roster of candidates (Nason 1998, 23). They also use consultants to screen candidates, conduct interviews, and check background information. Consultants know who and where the best candidates are. The most capable and desirable candidates are usually already employed; a consultant can actively recruit to ensure that the candidate pool is diverse and candidates are qualified, reputable, proven leaders.

It is important to find a good match between a consultant's services and the college's needs. Using probing interview questions in a "request-for-services" process can do this. Board members should pose questions such as the following to several potential vendors:

- What services will be provided? Developing a candidate profile? Advertising the position? Screening candidates? Checking references? What will be the cost?
- How will stakeholders be involved in needs assessment and candidate selection? In an advisory committee? In focus groups? In candidate interviews?
- What recruitment services will be used? Ads in journals? Phone calls?
- What training will be offered to board members? Will it cover such topics as legal issues and framing interview questions to elicit good information?
- What strategies will the consultant use to guarantee diversity in the candidate pool?

Trustees can negotiate costs in light of the services they desire. Above all, both the board and consultant need a clear and mutual understanding that although the steps of the process (developing a candidate profile, advertising the position, reviewing applications, interviewing candidates) are generally the same, the way in which those steps are implemented may vary. One way does not fit every situation. The consultant may suggest how to do it and, in fact, usually has developed proven successful procedures. But he or she must also be flexible—willing to advise, not to prescribe.

The ACC board used the same consultant in each of its two presidential searches; however, some significant changes in implementation were made in the second search, as described on the following pages.

Define the Role of the Board in the Search Process

Trustee leadership evolves. In ACC's first search, the board members had worked together for numerous years and enjoyed a good working relationship. There was a high degree of mutual trust. The board chair appointed three board members as a subcommittee to work with the consultant and report to the rest of the board.

By the time the second search was about to begin, four new members had joined the board. Board members had not worked together long enough to learn each other's values and to develop an easy and trustful working relationship. For that reason, in the second search, all nine members served on the Search Committee. This decision proved beneficial both to the board members and to the candidates. Reviewing the history, mission, and goals of the college resulted in commonly understood and supported principles. Board members learned about each other's personalities and decision-making styles; this familiarity created a more cordial and effective working relationship. All board members had a better understanding of the candidate pool and had ownership of the selection process.

Candidates observed board dynamics during preliminary and final interviews. Because the working relationship between the board and the president is critical for institutional success, it is better for candidates to learn in advance whether their own style of leadership would mesh with that of the board.

Reach a Consensus on the Compensation Package and Contract Terms

Well before the final negotiations begin, board members should discuss and develop a consensus on all terms of the contract to be offered and, when applicable, ensure that the consultant clearly informs candidates about them. This information includes salary range and benefits. The ACC board failed to finalize these details at the time of the first search. At that time, the board was also unaware of how competitive the outgoing president's salary and benefits package was in comparison with that of leaders in similar positions.

To ensure that ACC would be competitive in attracting good candidates at the time of the second search, the board reviewed the compensation packages of previous ACC presidents and of presidents of colleges equivalent to ACC, along with state and national comparisons to the local cost-of-living index. The board identified other benefits frequently included in presidential contracts and decided which ones ACC might offer to allow some flexibility in the compensation package. With the consultant's help, the board identified commonly used provisions relating to terms and conditions of employment. For example, it learned that most candidates would expect to have at least a three-year contract and would be unlikely to accept a one-year contract. The board also learned the contract would be expected to provide specifics about how and when the president would be evaluated. Resolving compensation issues ahead of time facilitated a quick agreement on contract terms after the board had made its choice of candidates.

Appoint a Diverse and Representative Search Advisory Committee

The standard procedure in a search is to appoint a Search Advisory Committee to the board. Great care should be taken in the selection of the members. The committee needs to reflect diverse points of view and yet be able to cooperate in achieving a common purpose.

The board appointed advisory committees in each of the two searches described in this chapter, but the committee membership was quite different. The 1993 Search Advisory Committee was largely internal. It consisted of nine members: three trustees, two faculty members, two business representatives, one ACC Foundation board representative, and one student. For the 1997 search, the board broadened the membership to 22 members to include more viewpoints. Nine trustees, five business community representatives (including a Chamber of Commerce member and a workforce training representative), four employee association representatives, two ACC Foundation board members, one university professor, and one student served on the committee. The expansion was largely mandated by the changes in community context between the two searches.

The board invited nominations and self-nominations but made it clear that the members selected would not be fervent advocates for a particular political constituency. The goal would be to choose members from various backgrounds to ensure a variety of viewpoints. Nominees would be expected to make a commitment to the institution as a whole, have tolerance for differing viewpoints, and be willing to work hard.

Each internal and external interest group in the community was invited to nominate at least three persons as its representative. Nominations were also solicited in local newspapers. From the nominee pool, the chair recommended and the board ratified specific appointees, resulting in a committee that reflected internal/external balance as well as equitable geographic, ethnic, age, and gender representation.

Define the Charge of the Search Committee

It is useless to appoint a committee unless the members feel they have meaningful roles and are confident that the board will listen to their advice. At the same time, the board cannot be expected to delegate the selection of the president-elect to a committee. This activity is the legal and proper province of the board. Therefore, before appointing the Search Advisory Committee, the board should deliberate, articulate, and declare an unequivocal charge to the committee.

The ACC board failed to do this during the first search. The result was confusion about the role of the committee on the part of board members and committee members. For the second search, the ACC board drafted a written Charge to the Presidential Search Advisory Committee that was signed by each member and posted on the Web site (see sidebar). The charge made it clear that the committee's role was advisory, and it specified the key functions that the group would be expected to play.

In addition to their shared responsibility, committee members had individual responsibilities. Each member would be expected to identify activities that the president should undertake in the first six months and to rank those activities in order of importance. Each member promised to identify groups and people with whom the president should meet and to assist with organizing the meetings and making introductions.

> **Charge to the Presidential Search Advisory Committee**
>
> ■ Participate in the first screening of written applications.
>
> ■ Participate in interviews.
>
> ■ Identify strengths and weaknesses of candidates, but do not rate them.
>
> ■ Recommend all qualified candidates to the trustees, who will confirm or reject the recommendations.
>
> ■ Develop and implement a transition plan for the new president.

Arm the Board with Data to Support Decision Making

There is no blueprint for college leadership; however, certain skills have been identified as important for effective presidents. These include the ability to bring a college together in the governing process. The ability to mediate, a good command of technology, a high level of tolerance for ambiguity, understanding of and appreciation for multiculturalism, and the ability to build coalitions are also important. In an

American Association of Community Colleges online survey, community college presidents indicated their belief that future presidents will need more entrepreneurial spirit and a more adaptive approach than presidents need today (Shults 2001, 8).

ACC used the 21st Century Educational Leadership Profile to assist in selecting candidates. After performing an environmental scan and securing input from the Search Advisory Committee, the ACC board identified three critical tasks for the new president: (1) to restore a balanced budget; (2) to resolve academic problems and restore the college to fully accredited status; and (3) to reestablish public confidence in and public support for the college through an aggressive public relations campaign.

The trustees asked the three finalists to self-administer the Occupational Personality Questionnaire, and their test results were sent to the director of the IHE for analysis. The college was furnished with a Person–Job Match Report for each candidate before the interviews.

This procedure affirmed judgments the trustees had already made about the candidates' strengths, weaknesses, and leadership styles, and the trustees entered the final decision-making phase confident that each of the finalists could effectively serve the college. The trustees also used the Leadership Profile to develop interview questions for candidates and for the people the candidates had listed as references. The trustees formed questions to elicit specific information that would or would not support the candidate's self-assessment. They included the following:

For the candidate:

What experience, if any, have you had in making difficult decisions where there was little time for extended deliberation? How did you handle it? If no experience, how would you handle it?

For the reference:

How receptive is the applicant to change? How effective is the candidate at handling multiple tasks?

The college has continued to use the Leadership Profile and similar tools for hiring administrators. Such analysis results in a stronger candidate pool and more cooperative teamwork at the administrative level.

Ensure Success with a Transition Plan

After a new president is appointed, some boards think their task is finished; in reality, the task is far from over. A significant act of leadership is planning a thoughtful entry period for the new president. Should they fail to do this, they make the common mistake of "dropping the president at the front gate" (AGB News 1995, 35). As one expert has said, it is "at the beginning of his tenure that the chief executive officer is most vulnerable—to criticism, pressure, long hours, unrealistic expectation, alienation from family, and the overriding concern that the CEO is ultimately responsible for everything that happens in an institution" (O'Banion 1989, 1).

Confident of having chosen the right person as a result of the first search, the ACC board did not volunteer to help with preparing the new president for his job. The results were unfortunate: when the president left after only three years, the trustees again faced the task of choosing a new president, this time in a troubled context, no doubt exacerbated by the board's failure to provide transition assistance.

Determined not to make the same mistake twice, the board spent significant time preparing a transition plan for the first year of the new president's tenure. Each board member pledged to support a plan developed to get the new president off to a good start. Key steps in this plan are summarized in the sidebar.

Creating and overseeing implementation of the transition plan were the responsibility of the Search Advisory Committee. Committee members were familiar with the president-elect's skills, were cognizant of the college's needs, and had the connections to community constituencies that were central to the success of the new president.

The transition plan ensured that the president would be introduced to the various stakeholder groups, would learn something of the institution's history, and would be advised about local political issues. A specific person was designated to ensure the meetings noted in the transition plan were completed.

A retreat for the board of trustees and the president was convened shortly after the president arrived. At this meeting, the board's expectations for the president were discussed and a calendar to review progress was created.

Conclusion

The American Association of Community Colleges reports that 45 percent of current presidents plan to retire by 2007, suggesting that more than 300 colleges will be undertaking presidential searches each year (Shults 2001, 1). Trustees must prepare themselves for this task. In addition to the all-important value of finding the right president, the search and selection process has three other advantages. First, it forces the institution to look at itself critically. Second, as they cooperate in a common cause, trustees, faculty, students, administrative officers, and others can increase their mutual understanding and trust. Finally, if done well, the choosing of a president can tell the institution's story to a wide audience in a way that will enhance the college's reputation. After finishing a search, board members should consider how they could do it better the next time. The board that has not conducted a search in the immediate past should plan contingency measures for the day when it will face this task.

References

Doser, Beatrice. 1991. "Effective Board/President Relations." *Trustee Quarterly* (summer): 6–10.

"Don't Drop the President at the Gate." 1995. *AGB News* (September/October): 35.

Maxwell, Earl. 1998. Letter to the ACC Search Committee, Austin Community College. Austin, Texas.

Nason, John W. 1998. "Responsibilities of the Governing Board." In *Handbook of College and University Trusteeship*, ed. Richard T. Ingram and Associates. San Francisco: Jossey-Bass.

O'Banion, Terry. 1989. "Retaining a Peak-Performing President." *Trustee Quarterly* (fall): 7–11.

Shults, Christopher. 2001. *The Critical Impact of Impending Retirements on Community College Leadership.* Research Brief Leadership Series, no. 1, AACC-RB-01-5. Washington, D.C.: American Association of Community Colleges.

Vaughan, George B. 1990. "How Long Is Too Long?" *Trustee Quarterly* (summer): 2–7.

CHAPTER 8

Leadership in Colleges Engaged in Quality Improvement

Dale F. Campbell, Professor and Director, Institute of Higher Education, University of Florida, and Barbara Sloan, Vice President, Academic Affairs, Tallahassee Community College

Community colleges, which enroll nearly six million credit students nationwide (U.S. Department of Education 2001), prospered in decades of dramatic growth. Now they are a major sector of higher education, and their leaders face new challenges. These challenges have emerged in part from a dramatic shift occurring as our society moves from an industrial-based to an information-based economy. Community colleges must be structured to be able to respond to a changed and changing environment (Rowley 2001; Vaughan 2000); they must be organized to address the factors of demand, competition, and quality (Alfred and Carter 2000); and they must be positioned to address the effects of globalization (Levin 2001). At the 2000 Community College Futures Assembly, community college faculty and administrators identified funding workforce development, using outcome measures for accountability, and meeting the cost of technology as critical issues facing their institutions (Campbell and Evans 2001). To meet these challenges successfully, community college leaders must adopt new organizational structures and develop a new understanding of leadership and the roles of leaders (Cain 1999; Pierce and Pedersen 1997; Tierney 1999).

Community colleges are seeking to define their roles and to focus on their core mission of teaching and learning. Schein (1992) states that leadership is the fundamental process by which organizational cultures are formed and changed. Many theorists believe that traditional views of leaders and leadership are unsuited to 21st-century organizations. Senge (1990), who described the organizational structure and characteristics needed for institutional learning, rejects the traditional view of the leader as a hero who sets the direction and makes key decisions. Instead, leaders should be designers, stewards, and teachers. O'Banion (1997) advocates the learning college, which is the antithesis of the hierarchical and authoritative models common to American educational institutions today. O'Banion (1997) states that to achieve a learning college, leaders must flatten their organizations, empower individuals, develop collaborative processes, commit to quality, and make learners of the stakeholders.

Traditionally, leadership studies have either focused on particular traits, behaviors, or situations or examined leaders or groups of leaders who have been perceived to be effective by other leaders or experts. Recently, however, leadership research has begun to address a combination of factors that include the situation, the leader, the followers, and the culture and structure of an organization (Yukl 2001). Factors affecting leadership include leadership traits, situational effects, and the interaction of traits and situation (Bass 1990). Yukl (2001) suggests that the various lines of research need to converge and that these diverse approaches should be viewed as part of a network of interacting variables.

This chapter describes the results of a case study of leaders in two colleges that have successfully implemented continuous quality improvement (CQI) in their institutions. Participants included the presidents of the two colleges and a total of 20 other leaders from the two institutions. The intent of the study was to look at several variables and their interactions within a particular leadership setting. The study explored leadership traits, styles, and behaviors of the presidents and their leadership teams, as well as situational and intervening factors present in institutions that have demonstrated effective implementation of CQI strategies.

Introduction and Methods

The two colleges' success in implementing continuous quality improvement was demonstrated by their involvement in a national CQI organization, by the results of a survey based on the 1998 Malcolm Baldrige Quality Award Education Criteria for Performance Excellence, by the receipt of awards and commendations, and by other evidence of successful CQI implementation.

Both quantitative and qualitative inquiry methods were used in this study. The Occupational Personality Questionnaire (OPQ) was used to determine the personality traits, leadership styles, and team types of the leaders. Questionnaires, institutional reports, and other documents were used to gather information about situational and intervening factors associated with successful implementation of CQI. Semistructured interviews were used to further explore the contextual conditions. To protect the identities of the presidents and the colleges, they are referred to as College One and President One and College Two and President Two.

For the purposes of this study, *situational variables* were identified as those contextual and organizational conditions that exist within a leadership setting. Researchers have identified three factors—the motivation for adopting CQI, organizational structure and culture, and the personal characteristics of leaders—as important situational factors to sustaining CQI (Van Allen 1994; Horine and Hailey 1995). *Personality traits* studied were determined by the three domains of the OPQ—relationships with people, thinking style, and feelings and emotions. OPQ data also yielded information on the *preferred leadership styles* of the leaders. The study explored each leader's preferences for five leadership styles (Bass 1990) and each leader's ability to adapt the use of those styles, depending on the circumstances. OPQ data were also used to determine preferred team types on the basis of Meredith Belbin's eight team roles for optimum performance (Saville & Holdsworth 1996).

Intervening variables were defined as those variables that mediate the effects of leadership behavior on end-result criteria of leadership success (Yukl 2001). In implementation of CQI, intervening variables are likely to include presidential commitment and involvement, follower commitment, training, and external events such as legislative or economic changes (Peterson 1993; Horine and Hailey 1995).

Both presidents wanted to improve colleges that were already considered successful. Neither implemented CQI as a response to a serious problem or crisis; however, College Two did experience a serious financial challenge in the early years of CQI implementation. As a result, President Two was challenged to maintain support for the resources needed to begin training and implementation of CQI at the same time that he had to find ways to provide funds to cover a three-year increase in faculty salaries that had followed a new union agreement.

Results

Situational Variables

The organizational structure of the colleges was defined on the basis of a review of internal documents, surveys, and interviews with the presidents. College One is a comprehensive community college that serves approximately 14,000 credit and 9,000 noncredit students each semester. It is part of a multicampus district, and its governance structure is determined by district policy. However, the district has expressed a commitment to quality principles, so the CQI structure and required employee participation at College One were not in conflict with the district's overall structure. College One has no faculty or staff unions, so the college does not have to participate in formal bargaining procedures. Employees in all areas of the college are involved in CQI and are focused on student learning, and the college's processes are grounded in the Baldrige Criteria for Education. The president has embraced the concept of the learning college and of leadership in which leaders and followers exert mutual influence. The college uses cross-functional teams and horizontal work structures.

College Two is a single-campus district that serves a vast geographic area. It serves approximately 27,500 credit and 15,000 noncredit students each semester. The faculty and staff are represented by three unions, and formal bargaining is an integral part of the governance structure. In addition, state law mandates some parts of the governance structure. Governance involves the interaction of a number of entities, including the executive management team, the academic and classified staff senates, bargaining units, local union chapters, campus committees, the faculty association, student government, and the board of trustees.

Even though the organizational structure of the college is in part mandated by state law, the president has created cross-functional teams and process-improvement teams that cut horizontally across the structure. The college has more than 30 standing committees or subcommittees whose purpose is to review or oversee all areas of the college and to make recommendations for policy and procedure development and modification. In addition, the college has aligned its nine critical systems with the seven Baldrige Criteria for Education. The president has used these criteria to frame a systems approach for the college's critical functions.

Implementation of CQI at College One began with a leader who had served as the college's president for more than 10 years and had worked at the college since its beginning. He had extensive involvement in shaping the organization and culture of the college before he began implementing CQI. President Two also had more than 10 years' experience as a president when he began implementing CQI; however, he was new to College Two. He began implementation in a culture that existed when he arrived.

Despite the differences indicated above, the leaders in this study influenced their institutions in similar ways. Both presidents were involved in the process from the beginning, and they continue to be the primary force for CQI in their institutions. Ten years after they began implementation, they remain committed to continuous improvement. Both involved their senior leadership teams early in the implementation process. The leadership teams have fully integrated a planning and assessment cycle using the Baldrige Criteria for Education. They have invested time and resources to provide training and ongoing support; they have developed a system of teams to implement their goals; and they have remained sensitive to the effects of change on the college's culture by adjusting training and implementation as needed.

Personality Attributes of the College Leaders

The OPQ includes 30 attributes of personality grouped in three domains: (1) Relationships with People; (2) Thinking; and (3) Feelings and Emotions. For this study, the two presidents and a total of 20 members of their leadership teams were administered the OPQ. President One identified 14 individuals who make up his leadership team; all completed the OPQ. President Two identified nine leaders, six of whom completed the OPQ.

Of the 30 attributes, the two presidents' scores were consistent on 14 attributes (46.7 percent), including the Socially Confident scale. Their scores are similar on another eight attributes (Figure 8.1). They differed on nine attributes (30 percent).

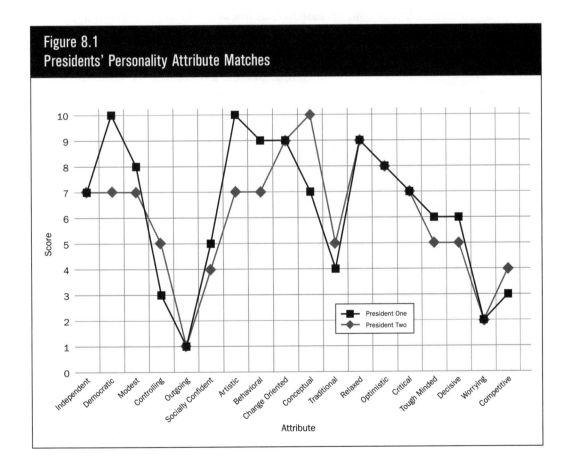

Figure 8.1
Presidents' Personality Attribute Matches

The following analysis describes the relationship of the presidents' attributes to a high level of CQI implementation. A CQI environment requires a president who supports a shared decision-making process. These presidents scored high on Independent. They are willing to share their views, even if unpopular, and to express opinions even when contrary to a team's view. The presidents are also Democratic, encouraging others to participate and listening and consulting with others. These two attributes in combination contribute to broad-based participation. The high level of the Modest attribute is also relevant to CQI. This attribute indicates that the leaders treat everyone equally, that they deemphasize status, and that they share credit for successes. These leaders are not Controlling; they seek input from groups and individuals rather than take charge and give instructions. The presidents scored low on Outgoing. Rather than being extroverted and commanding the center of attention, these leaders are reserved and avoid the limelight, leaving room for others to shine. They scored in the moderate range on Socially Confident. They are able to put people at ease and are comfortable in new situations, but not to such a degree that they become the dominant personality in social groups.

Of the 20 other leaders who participated in the study in the two institutions, 15 also had a high score on the Independent attribute. Most also scored in the medium-to-high range on Modest and Democratic. Four scored low on the Modest attribute, and three scored low on the Democratic attribute. Most scored in the medium range on Outgoing; three scored in the low range. Both presidents emphasized the importance of shared leadership, listening to others, and encouraging self-directed teams; that is, they minimize the importance of the single leader and stress instead the importance of each individual's role in leadership.

In the Thinking domain, the two presidents scored in the high range on the Artistic, Behavioral, Change Oriented, and Conceptual attributes. Because CQI involves continous change, leaders in CQI institutions should be highly Change Oriented; these presidents accept change and seek out new approaches. This attribute is combined with a moderate tendency for Traditional. When interviewed, both presidents displayed sensitivity to those who resist change and who are uncomfortable with the unknown. Both had adapted their implementation of CQI to account for these individuals or groups.

The presidents said they enjoy the creative aspects of change, as indicated in their high Artistic scores. Both also enjoy analyzing and understanding the behaviors of others, and both are conceptual thinkers who enjoy working with theories. These attributes enable them to monitor both the human and technical aspects of the total quality philosophy. All of these attributes are consistent with implementing a new system such as CQI and with introducing change, empowering others, and maintaining a system that is continuously changing.

Of the 20 other leaders, 17 also scored in the medium-to-high range on Artistic. At least 70 percent of these leaders scored in the medium-to-high range on Behavioral and Conceptual. As a group, the other leaders were somewhat less likely than were the presidents to engage in studying the behavior of others or in theoretical thinking.

The other leaders were fairly evenly distributed in their scores on Traditional, but only two scored low on the Change Oriented attribute. Overall, the presidents and the other leaders balance introducing and embracing change with recognizing and valuing the traditional.

The presidents differed on three attributes that seem important to an organization committed to the principles and assessments of CQI, and particularly to alignment with the Baldrige criteria. These are the Data Rational, Forward Planning, and Detail Conscious attributes. President One scored in the low range on all three, but President Two scored in the high range. A high score on Data Rational is consistent with the emphasis on use of data in CQI. President One indicated that he had come to have a reluctant respect for data, although he gets no particular satisfaction from dealing with it. He prefers that decisions be influenced, rather than driven, by data. President One is much less likely to be involved in planning or in the details of a plan than is President Two. A continuous improvement organization requires careful assessment and planning processes. President One indicated that over the past 20 years he has empowered others and has delegated many responsibilities. He said that he understands the need for these activities, but that he is much less directly involved in them than he was in the past.

The profiles of the 14 other leaders in College One indicate that 12 have a moderate-to-high tendency to possess the Data Rational attribute and 10 have a moderate-to-high tendency to possess the Forward Planning and Detail Conscious attributes. Thus, the president can evidently rely on the interests and abilities of other college leaders in these areas.

In the domain of Feelings and Emotions, the presidents' scores are similar on seven of the 10 attributes. Both scored high on three attributes: Relaxed, Optimistic, and Critical. They scored in the midrange on Tough Minded and Decisive, and in the low range on Worrying and Competitive. Both presidents expressed great optimism and confidence in their quality journeys. In an atmosphere of continuous assessment and change, optimism and confidence are needed qualities. Their optimism is combined with a tendency to be critical, to probe the facts, and to critically assess plans and processes. The presidents displayed a moderate level of the Decisive attribute. They are able to make decisions even if all the facts are not available, but they avoid hasty or risky decision making. Neither president is particularly competitive. Both expressed a desire to develop self-directed teams and to involve all members of the community in decision making. Their emphasis on being involved rather than on being competitive promotes this philosophy. The presidents are moderately Tough Minded. They are not insensitive, but they are able to accept criticism and negative feedback in order to sustain continuous improvement.

Of the 20 other leaders, two scored low on Relaxed and on Optimistic and three scored low on Critical. Four scored high on the Worrying attribute. Overall, the other leaders tended to be calm and optimistic like the presidents. Only two scored high on Competitive, but nine fell in the medium range, suggesting that the other leaders are somewhat more competitive than the presidents.

Leadership Styles

The OPQ measures five leadership styles—Directive, Delegative, Participative, Consultative, Negotiative—plus the ability to adapt one's use of the styles. Despite the large number of attributes that the presidents have in common, the application of those attributes in leadership situations appears quite different (Figure 8.2). President One favors Participative and Consultative styles and is unlikely to use the Directive style. He wants to make sure that everyone's views are heard and that decisions are agreed on by the group. He is highly likely to gather opinions from others and to involve others in the decision-making processes.

President Two, on the other hand, has a moderate tendency for all of the styles. The situational variables in College Two may contribute to the president's use of a variety of styles. For example, President Two might use a Participative or Consultative style when interacting with his leadership team but may be more likely to Negotiate or be Directive when interacting with unions or within state-mandated structures. Both presidents scored high on the Adaptability scale, indicating a high capacity to adopt different styles of behavior in different circumstances.

As a group, the 14 other leaders in College One have a moderate tendency to use all of the styles. Like the president, most of them have a high or moderate ability to be adaptable. All the other leaders in College Two fall in the medium range for all five leadership styles. Like their president, they tend to use all of the styles, although all of them are less adaptable than the president.

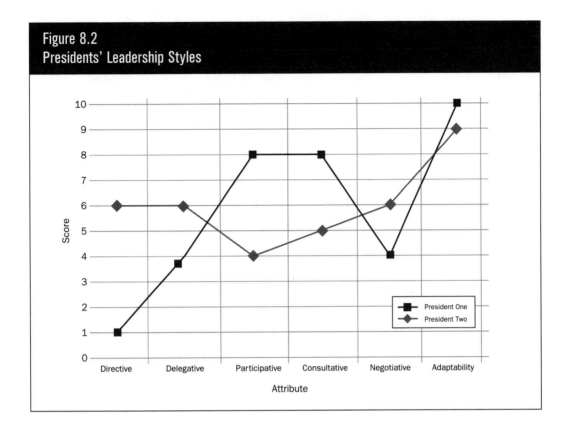

Figure 8.2
Presidents' Leadership Styles

Team Types

The OPQ also analyzes responses in relation to eight team types. Belbin (2000) suggests that effective teams include individuals who serve differing roles. The two presidents share some characteristics but differ on others (see Figure 8.3). Both are unlikely to play the role of Shaper, a person who tends to take charge and to persuade the team to accept his or her personal objectives. Both are likely to serve as a team's Innovator and Monitor/Evaluator. Innovators are creative and resourceful and introduce new ideas. In the role of Monitor/Evaluator, the presidents are likely to remain detached and to evaluate and summarize the team's efforts.

President One is likely to be the Team Worker, and President Two may also play that role. As Team Workers, the presidents are likely to use their sensitivity and caring traits to keep the team functioning and to minimize interpersonal problems among team members.

The other leaders in both colleges exhibited a great deal of diversity in the team roles they are likely to play. In College One, 10 of the 14 other leaders scored in the high range for the role of Monitor/Evaluator, and 9 were in the medium range as Team Worker. The rest of the scores were widely distributed, from low to high, on

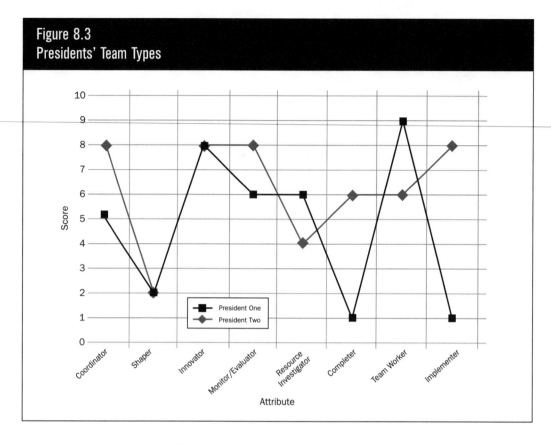

Figure 8.3
Presidents' Team Types

the other six team types. This is the kind of diversity that President One indicated that he values. President One's high score as Team Worker makes him well suited to coordinate a team of this type.

In College Two, individuals tended to score in the medium range for most of the team types whereas the president scored in the high range on half of them. For example, five of the six other leaders were in the medium range for Monitor/Evaluator, and no leaders were in the high range. Similarly, no leaders from this college were in the high range as Completer, and only one scored in the high range on Implementer. On the other hand, two scored in the medium range and two in the high range on Resource Investigator, thus filling a role where the president scored low.

Intervening Variables

A final area of inquiry was intervening variables that might affect implementation and continuation of CQI in the institution. The intervening variables identified in the literature as important to implementation were presidential commitment and involvement, follower commitment, training, and external events that may affect the college.

Both presidents provided the vision for implementing CQI, and both were the catalysts for planning and implementation. Both presidents are strongly committed to the concepts and continue to be directly involved in continuous improvement.

Both presidents have provided extensive opportunities for individuals to learn about and practice CQI principles through workshops and training sessions. Both indicated that they have adapted the training to fit the situation.

Although they continue to be involved in CQI, both presidents stated that the responsibility for continuous improvement belongs to all members of the college community. President One indicated that all employees share the responsibility for continuously improving their areas of primary responsibility. President Two stressed the importance of self-directed teams in the CQI structure.

Both presidents continuously monitor the change process and maintain the disciplined approach of the CQI process even when external events such as budget cuts or external governance changes occur. Both presidents have continued their quality journeys through economic downturns, personnel turnovers, and other changes.

Conclusion

This study examined the situational and intervening variables, the personality attributes, leadership styles, and team types of the presidents and their leadership teams in two colleges that have received recognition for their work in implementing CQI and applying the Baldrige criteria in their colleges. The examination of multiple criteria provides a broader understanding of leadership traits, situational effects, and the interaction of traits and situation.

For practitioners, this study provides some insight into how a leader's attributes relate to his or her leadership situation and to other leaders within the institution. The two presidents and their leadership teams exhibit many qualities that are traditionally associated with effective leadership, as described by authors such as Vaughan (1986); Fisher, Tack, and Wheeler

> The examination of multiple criteria provides a broader understanding of leadership traits, situational effects, and the interaction of traits and situation.

(1988); Roueche, Baker, and Rose (1988); Hammons and Keller (1990); Fisher and Koch (1996); and Campbell and Leverty (1997). However, there are differences as well. For example, high levels of the Controlling and Competitive attributes or a low level of the Traditional attribute are not suited to the CQI environment. Differences may be attributed to the specific leadership situation or to the interaction of the presidents with other leaders on their college teams whose traits may complement those of the president.

This study suggests that those who select, orient, and develop new leaders should take into account the leadership situation and the organizational and cultural variables present in an institution. The study also suggests that the attributes and abilities of all team members should be studied. Leadership training should include an understanding of other leaders in the college and of the interactions between and among leaders.

References

Alfred, R., and P. Carter. 2000. "Contradictory Colleges: Thriving in an Era of Continuous Change." *New Expeditions: Charting the Second Century of Community Colleges.* Issues Paper No. 6. (ERIC Document Reproduction Service No. ED 439 738.)

Bass, B. M. 1990. *Bass and Stogdill's Handbook of Leadership: Theory, Research, and Managerial Applications.* 3d ed. New York: Free Press.

Belbin, R. M. 2000. *Beyond the Team.* Oxford: Butterworth-Heinemann.

Cain, M. S. 1999. *The Community College in the Twenty-First Century. A Systems Approach.* Lanham, Md.: University Press of America.

Campbell, D. F., and R. Evans. 2001. "Quality Learning Communities: It's Commitment That Counts." *Community College Journal of Research and Practice* 25(1): 1–4.

Campbell, D. F., and L. H. Leverty. 1997. "Developing and Selecting Leaders for the 21st Century." *Community College Journal* 67(4): 34–36.

Fisher, J. L., and James V. Koch. 1996. *Presidential Leadership: Making a Difference.* Phoenix, Ariz.: American Council on Education and Oryx Press.

Fisher, J. L., M. W. Tack, and K. Wheeler. 1988. *The Effective College President.* New York: Macmillan.

Hammons, J. O., and L. Keller. 1990. "Competencies and Personal Characteristics of Future Community College Presidents." *Community College Review* 18(3): 34–41.

Horine, J. E., and W. A. Hailey. 1995. "Challenges to Successful Quality Management Implementation in Higher Education Institutions." *Innovative Higher Education* 20(1): 7–17.

Levin, J. S. 2001. *Globalizing the Community College: Strategies for Change in the Twenty-First Century*. New York: Palgrave.

O'Banion, T. 1997. *A Learning College for the 21st Century*. Phoenix, Ariz.: Oryx Press.

Peterson, C. S. 1993. "Continuous Quality Assurance: Adapting TQM for Community Colleges." (ERIC Document Reproduction Service No. ED 356 016.)

Pierce, D. R., and R. D. Pedersen. 1997. "The Community College Presidency: Qualities for Success." In *Presidents and Trustees in Partnership: New Roles and Leadership Challenges*. No. 98. New Directions for Community Colleges, eds. I. M. Weisman and G. B. Vaughan. San Francisco: Jossey-Bass; 13–19.

Roueche, J. E., G. A. Baker III, and R. R. Rose. 1988. "The Community College President as Transformational Leader." *AACJC Journal* 58(5): 48–52.

Rowley, D. J. 2001. *From Strategy to Change: Implementing the Plan in Higher Education*. Higher and Adult Education Series. San Francisco: Jossey-Bass.

Saville and Holdsworth Ltd. 1996. *Occupational Personality Questionnaire Manual and User's Guide*. Boston: SHL.

Schein, E. H. 1992. *Organizational Culture and Leadership*. 2d ed. San Francisco: Jossey-Bass.

Senge, P. M. 1990. *The Fifth Discipline: The Art and Practice of the Learning Organization*. New York: Doubleday.

Tierney, W. G. 1999. *Building the Responsive Campus: Creating High-Performance Colleges and Universities*. Thousand Oaks, Calif.: Sage.

U.S. Department of Education. 2001. "Projections of College Enrollment, Degrees Conferred, and High School Graduates, 2000–2011." *The Chronicle of Higher Education, Almanac Issue* 48(1): 22.

Van Allen, G. H. 1994. "Failures of Total Quality Management: Products of Leadership and Organizational Culture." *Community College Journal of Research and Practice* 18(4): 381–390.

Vaughan, G. B. 1986. *The Community College Presidency*. New York: Macmillan.

——. 2000. *The Community College Story*. 2d ed. Washington, D.C.: Community College Press, American Association of Community Colleges.

Yukl, G. 2001. *Leadership in Organizations*. 3d ed. Upper Saddle River, N.J.: Prentice Hall.

CHAPTER 9

Recommendations for Executive Development and Selection

Dale F. Campbell, Professor and Director, Institute of Higher Education, University of Florida

This chapter presents guidance for those interested in participating in or launching community college leadership-development efforts. Following are specific recommendations, a description of a model leadership program with a sample curriculum for a certificate in community college executive leadership, a sample memo to the board of trustees, and a list of selected national resources. As with the other chapters, these suggestions are not exhaustive but are meant to raise awareness and encourage planning and action.

Recommendations for Leadership Development

Recommendations for Trustees

Policy. Adopt or reaffirm the board's commitment to professional development.

Investment. Invest in leadership development, even in tight fiscal times.

Succession Planning. Establish a process for conducting executive searches before positions become vacant.

Leadership Team Audit. Conduct an audit of the preferred leadership styles and competencies of your college's current executive officers before beginning an executive search.

Recommendations for Presidents

Encouragement. Encourage promising individuals to explore the challenges and rewards of a career as a community college administrator.

Value. Make development of the college faculty and staff a priority for your cabinet and leadership team.

Support. Provide funding for tuition reimbursement or matching funds for employees pursuing a doctorate in community college administration and for employee participation in American Association of Community Colleges (AACC) Presidents Academy institutes or other leadership development programs.

Leadership Development and Mentoring. Establish a leadership development program at your college.

Recommendations for Potential Leaders

Passion. If you have a passion for making a difference in people's lives, talk with key leaders about the challenges and rewards of a career in community college administration.

Exploration. Explore your interest by enrolling in graduate classes in community college administration.

Commitment. Make a commitment to pursue and earn a doctorate in community college administration.

Investment. Be willing to invest your own funds to participate in community college professional organization leadership programs and conferences.

Recommendations for University Graduate Programs

Priority. Make overcoming the leadership gap for community college administrators a priority of your graduate faculty, dean, and president.

Partnerships. Reach out to community colleges as they establish their leadership development programs.

Certification. Award a certificate in community college executive leadership.

Model Leadership Program

A one-year executive leadership certificate could be offered through a university in cooperation with a host community college or more than one community college. The graduate credit program would be designed for career entry or professional upgrade. Credits would be applicable to further graduate study and would be recognized by the sponsoring community college(s) when they consider applicants for future executive officer positions. Figure 9.1 shows a sample curriculum for the certificate.

Figure 9.1
Sample Curriculum for Certificate in Community College Executive Leadership

Summer Semester
Higher Education Administration (3)
Colloquium in Community College Leadership (1)

Fall Semester
Practicum/Mentorship in Community College Administration (3)
Community College in America (3)
Colloquium in Community College Leadership (1)

Spring Semester
Higher Education Electives (6)
Colloquium in Community College Leadership (1)

Recommended Electives
Diversity Issues in Higher Education (3)
Financing of Higher Education (3)
The Law and Higher Education (3)

Total   18 Semester Hours

The colloquium experience would be based on an individual assessment using the 21st Century Educational Leadership Profile and the OPQ. Upon receiving their individual assessment report, graduate students would develop learning plans and a contract to strengthen identified areas of notable difference between the individual's current preferred work style and the profile of the 21st century educational leader.

For example, if the attributes a student wishes to develop include becoming more "socially confident," "outgoing," and "affiliative," the student might choose to join Toastmasters International to accomplish the learning objectives. The contract requires that students outline specific learning activities and readings, and it requires regular feedback on progress in achieving the objectives to the university professor, community college executive officer mentor, and fellow leadership program partici-pants. This feedback provides a supportive learning environment with high expecta-tions for students to achieve their learning goals.

Memo to the Board

Community college presidents may wish to encourage their board of trustees to sup-port a leadership development program at the college. Figure 9.2 illustrates a board action item from "Learning Community College" (LCC), which could serve as a model.

Leadership Development Resources

Following are examples of established resources available for community college leadership development.

American Association of Community Colleges

AACC Presidents Academy. All AACC member CEOs are automatically members of the AACC Presidents Academy. The academy's Summer Institute focuses on team building, problem solving, and renewal. The Technology Leadership Institute, also held during the summer, focuses on enhancing IT awareness and solutions. The fall DC Institute gives presidents an opportunity to learn more about federal government relations and to visit leaders on Capitol Hill.

Professional Development Leadership Database of University Leadership Programs for Community College Administrators, www.aacc.nche.edu/ leadership. This database on the AACC Web site is searchable by state, degrees offered, availability of internships and financial aid, curriculum, and residency requirements. The site provides detailed information on specific programs and names of contact persons.

AACC Affiliate Councils

A number of AACC affiliate councils offer leadership development programs for their members. Examples include the Hispanic Council, the Black American Affairs

Figure 9.2
Board Action Item

Issue: Pending executive cabinet member retirements at Learning Community College and projected national shortage of community college leaders.

Recommendation: Establish a leadership program in cooperation with a university community college leadership doctoral program.

Background and Rationale: Nearly half of the more than 1,200 community college presidents nationally will be retiring in the next six years. One-fourth or more of these colleges' other chief administrators will retire in the next five years. Additional skills that CEOs will need in the future include greater flexibility, an understanding of technology, and the ability to seek business and industry partnerships. New LCC cabinet members will need these skills, as well as a commitment to the community college philosophy of extending access and valuing diversity.

■ The proposed leadership institute curriculum includes these areas, and it features the latest in research. Applicants accepted into the program will work directly with a mentor on the cabinet outside their normal area of responsibility. Individuals who complete the one-year program will be awarded a certificate in community college executive management by the partnering university. Some individuals may decide to apply for admission to the university to complete their doctoral program. LCC will support these individuals through our existing professional development fund under which we match the employee's contribution toward completing an advanced degree in his or her field of study or another approved area.

Alternatives

■ Use existing LCC's existing executive search processes, under which LCC invites applications when position openings occur.

■ Increase tuition reimbursement by 50 percent to 100 percent for selected staff to complete their doctoral programs in community college leadership.

■ Establish a leadership program in cooperation with a university community college leadership doctoral program.

Cost: $90,000. The cost includes graduate tuition and fees at $250 per credit hour for a one-year certificate program for 20 members of the LCC faculty and staff.

Value-Added Outcomes: Twenty LCC faculty and staff will be prepared to assume greater leadership responsibilities within one year. This program will ensure that the college has a pool of internal applicants from whom to draw when leadership vacancies occur. This program will also communicate the board's commitment to learning by helping prepare LCC staff and faculty for challenges the institution will face in a more competitive marketplace.

Roundtable, the Council for Resource Development, the Community College Business Officers Council, and the National Council on Student Development. Leadership development programs offered through the councils are often designed to assist new or aspiring executive officers in their leadership roles. Senior executive officers work with participants and encourage networking and sharing of best practices.

Other National Organizations

A number of other community college organizations, including the League for Innovation in the Community College and The Chair Academy of the Maricopa Community College District in Arizona, sponsor leadership development programs.

21st Century Educational Leadership Profile

As described throughout this book, the 21st Century Educational Leadership Profile developed by the Institute of Higher Education (IHE), University of Florida, and Saville & Holdsworth, Ltd., enables colleges to assess potential candidates' work styles. Candidates for leadership positions may consent to take an online self-assessment questionnaire designed to provide information on preferred work styles. IHE analyzes the results for colleges, providing a tool for evaluating top candidates and for developing interview questions. Colleges may also use the results to create individual learning plans for college administrators.

Conclusion

With thoughtful planning, community colleges can meet the leadership challenge. Many colleges have already instituted leadership development programs and recognize that they will need to continue to refine their plans and experiment with new strategies to find those best suited to their institution. This book presents a number of model strategies colleges have employed to enhance their leadership programs. The lessons shared here represent a range of challenges and situations colleges might face as they seek to fill a growing number of vacancies and cultivate strong, effective leaders. Working collaboratively and sharing such model programs, the nation's community colleges can successfully close the leadership gap.

INDEX

compensation package and contract terms, 72–73

data for decision making, 74–75

environmental scan and, 68–69

news media and, 69–70

professional consultants, 70–71

recommendations for executive development and selection, 93–98

Search Advisory Committee and, 73–74

transition plan, 76–77

uniqueness of each search, 68–69

Presidents Academy institutes, AACC, 96

professional consultants, presidential searches and, 70–71

Profiles Project. *See* 21st Century Educational Leadership Profiles Project

R

recruitment. *See also* presidential searches

client-based service delivery model, 61

diversity and, 59–66

electronic applications, 64

faculty biographies and, 62

internal sources and networks and, 61–63

Internet and, 64

Occupational Personality Questionnaire and, 64–66

quality-of-life issues, 60–61

traditional techniques, 59–60

tried-and-true methods and, 61

21st Century Educational Leadership Profile and, 64–66

resources, leadership development, 96–98

Retention Task Force, Daytona Beach Community College, 40–41

Roueche, John, 31

S

Saville & Holdsworth Ltd., 4–14, 98

shared governance, 15–17, 18, 20

SHL. *See* Saville & Holdsworth Ltd.

Show Time at High Noon Series, 60

Situational Leadership Workshops, Daytona Beach Community College, 38–39

Staub Leadership Consultants' Helping Individuals Lead Successfully (HILS) Seminar, 22

T

Taylor, Frederick Winslow, task analysis methods, 48

The Chair Academy of the Maricopa Community College District (Arizona) 98

Tri-C. See Cuyahoga Community College (Ohio)

21st Century Educational Leadership Profile

Austin Community College use of, 75

colloquium experience, 95–96

Daytona Beach Community College's Beacon Leadership Program and, 37

individual development and, 22

Macomb Community College test of, 53–55

Parkland College use of, 31

recruitment and, 64–66

Subordinate Behavior category, 18

21st Century Educational Leadership Profiles Project. *See also* Occupational Personality Questionnaire

Attribute-Based Person–Job Match Report, 5

first phase, 5–14

gender studies, 8–9

internal validity and, 10

limitations, 9–10

mean scores, community college administrators, 8

participants, 5, 7

positions held by participants, 7

purpose, 4

results, 7–9

User's Group meetings, 6

U

University of Florida

Educational Leadership, Policy, and Foundations Department, 38

Institute of Higher Education's 21st Century Educational Leadership Profiles Project, 4–14, 98

V

Vaughan, George, 27

 Dale F. Campbell is professor and director of the Institute of Higher Education at the University of Florida. His current research interests include the development of the 21st Century Educational Leadership Profile, a work profile for executive selection and development. He is the author of numerous publications relating to community colleges and leadership development. He received the 2000 Leadership Award from the American Association of Community Colleges (AACC).

In 1995, Campbell founded the Community College Futures Assembly and Bellwether Awards, an independent national policy forum to identify critical issues facing community colleges and recognize model trendsetting programs. He was also instrumental in founding the Community College Business Officers, an affiliate council of AACC, for which he serves as executive director emeritus.

Campbell was previously assistant commissioner for community and technical colleges at the Texas Higher Education Coordinating Board and visiting professor of educational administration at the University of Texas at Austin. He has also served as assistant professor and coordinator of the Community College Education Program at North Carolina State University; dean of instruction, Wichita Falls for Vernon Regional Junior College in Texas; and head of the Public and Support Services Department, Community College of the Air Force.

Campbell holds a B.A. degree in secondary education from the University of North Carolina at Chapel Hill, an M.A. in higher education from Appalachian State University, and a Ph.D. in educational administration from the University of Texas at Austin.